A NATURALISTIC THEORY OF JUSTICE
Critical Commentary on, and Selected Readings from, C.I. Lewis' Ethics

Vincent Luizzi
Southwestern Center for Value Studies
Southwest Texas State University

To My Parents

Preface

This book is designed to acquaint the reader with C.I. Lewis' ethics by providing critical commentary on Lewis' work in addition to reprinting some of Lewis' writings in ethics. The commentary is not meant to be a substitute for the complete work in ethics that Lewis was preparing before his death but merely a systematic study of some central aspects of his thought in ethics.

The selections do overlap somewhat, and the issues contained therein do not always follow in the order in which they are presented in the commentary. These infelicities are primarily the result of an attempt to realize two important goals — choosing selections that both represent Lewis' general views in ethics and supply the reader with primary source material on a number of the specific topics discussed in the critical commentary.

Permission to reprint "The Rational Imperatives" was purchased for $90.00 from Rutgers University Press. That essay of Lewis' appeared in *Vision & Action: Essays in Honor of Horace M. Kallen on his 70th Birthday*, edited by Sidney Ratner, copyright 1953 by the Trustees of Rutgers College in New Jersey. Permission to reprint passages from Lewis' *The Ground and Nature of the Right* was purchased for $90.00 from Columbia University Press which holds the 1955 copyright. Finally, permission to reprint Lewis' "The Individual and the Social Order" was purchased for $125.00 from Stanford University Press. The full acknowledgment appears on the page where this article begins, as per an aggreement with Stanford University Press.

TABLE OF
CONTENTS

CRITICAL COMMENTARY

SELECTED READINGS

CHAPTER 1
INTRODUCTORY REMARKS

I

C. I. Lewis' output in the field of ethics in one sense stands in striking contrast to his commitment that ethics is "the most important branch of philosophy."[1] For we find, on the one hand, that the Harvard pragmatist, who was trained by Royce and James, made systematic and substantial contributions to metaphysics, epistemology, value theory, and logic between 1929 and 1945 with his *Mind and the World Order* (hereafter *MWO*), *An Analysis of Knowledge and Valuation* (*AKV*), and *Symbolic Logic* (co-authored by Langford). Yet, by Lewis' own admission in 1960, his published books in ethics — *The Ground and Nature of the Right* (*GNR*) and *Our Social Inheritance* (*OSI*) — only indicate "something of the direction in which I think that I must move here."[2]

From another point of view, however, we can understand Lewis' attempts in ethics as drawing heavily on his earlier works that he thought propaedeutic to any study of ethics. Indeed, Lewis tells us that after he completed *MWO* and *Symbolic Logic* in 1929, he began to direct his attention to ethics but found that, *inter alia*, "the most important impediment to these studies in ethics was that I shortly came to recognize that the ethical conceptions of which I was convinced required the premise that objective and valid valuations represent a species of empirical knowledge."[3] It was in *AKV* that Lewis developed this thesis which he considered essential for furthering his main project of combining a form of Kantianism with tenets of utilitarian ethical theory.[4] Now, Lewis did address himself to these issues in a wide range of talks and essays, some unpublished until recently. Moreover, Professor Lange tells us that when Lewis died, Lewis' shelves "were lined with dozens of notebooks, containing innumerable drafts and studies for his final work, a major contribution to ethics. . . .There are approximately 9,500 pages of handscript in the most recent notebooks, the substantial majority of which is devoted to the projected work on ethics."[5]

Against this backdrop it seems there is a clear need for studies directed at integrating, criticizing, and extending Lewis' unfinished project in ethics. In what follows, I organize the material not to effect a historical exposition of Lewis' ideas in ethics but to bring us closer to realizing Lewis' goals and to do

1

this in a way that preserves the major categories of thought that permeate Lewis' ethical theory. Accordingly, Lewis' overall view of imperatives is entertained along with a careful consideration of those of primary importance for his ethics — the ethical and the prudential. Although the demands of prudence might be properly thought of as lying outside those of the moral, their interrelations with the moral are many, and, as we shall see throughout, any proper consideration of the moral turns on one of the prudential. To make clearer why the study has been structured along these lines, and as a further introduction to the ethics, some general observations should be made of Lewis' ethical theory, of its relation to his value theory, and of his moral imperative.

First, we should take notice of a primary motive of Lewis' for developing his ethical theory. Lewis was deeply disturbed by the skeptical challenges of his day that undermined what he found so important:

> In all the world and in all of life there is nothing more important to determine than what is right. . . .We live, however, in an age of skepticism. . . .Men have become doubtful of any bedrock for firm belief, any final ground for unhesitant action, of any principles not relative to circumstance or colored by personal feeling or affected by persuasions which may be only temporary and local. And in this period, as in other and like epochs in history, doubts are voiced whether the distinction of right and wrong, in one or another of its modes, is other than subjective or has any fixed and final sense.[6]

It is no distortion of Lewis' ethics to say that he viewed the skeptic as an ongoing antagonist. In fact, his enterprise in ethics can be seen as an answer to the skeptical challenge of logical positivists like A.J. Ayer, contemporaries of Lewis' whom he undoubtedly saw as his foes. And viewing Lewis' work in this way allows us to lay on the table a fundamental relationship between his ethics and value theory as well as the limits of his value theory in handling ethical problems.

Against skeptical claims like Ayer's that judgments such as "Stealing is wrong" and "Giving to charity is good" have emotive meaning only and at most serve to direct the attitudes of others,[7] Lewis waged a two-fold attack.

2

On the one hand, he developed a value theory resting on an epistemology that allowed him to deal with value judgments, such as "Giving to charity is good," as any other cognitive empirical claim. On the other, Lewis' effort was one of arguing that imperatives governing correct thinking and doing pervade human experience and that the moral critique (or set of moral rules), which allows us, in part, to judge that some act, like stealing, is wrong, occupies a status as legitimate in human experience as the rules of logic which allow us to judge that "if P, then Q; Q; therefore P" is wrong.

Lewis' value theory, then, handles assessments of good and bad, his ethics, of moral right and wrong. While the value theory allows us to make various judgments of what is empirically good, all we have is a set of predictions of what activity can lead to satisfying experiences or what Lewis refers to as being immediately valuable; for each objective value claim, on Lewis' view, strictly implies a set of predictions that if certain conditions are met, satisfactions accrue. And at this point no peculiarly ethical issues involving what is right and wrong are raised. As a matter of fact, Lewis points out that moral theorists of divergent persuasions might well agree on determinations of value, thus underlining his view that questions of value and of ethical correctness are distinct. The utilitarian and the egoist, for example, who are chiefly concerned with what is of value to society and the individual, respectively, both deal with questions of empirical or non-moral value and can reach agreement between themselves as to what is of individual value and what is of social value.

> There is no reason, for example, why an egoist
> in ethics and an uncompromising social utili-
> tarian should disagree over the question what *is*
> in the interests of the individual and what *is* for
> the best of all concerned.[8]

But, again, on the question of what good one *should* pursue, the value theory makes no claims. And similarly, the value theory provides no answers for how goods of social value are to be ordered. Now, this is not to say that the tenets of Lewis' theories of value and of right never intertwine. It is his rules of prudence and of justice that jointly advise us what goods we ought to pursue. More specifically, of those things we know to be of value, these rules advise which we ought to seek and which are permissible to seek.

II

Although we will pay particular attention to the moral imperative in Chapter 4, no introductory remarks on Lewis' ethics could be complete without some exposition of what the moral imperative demands, where it came from, and what some of its distinctive features are. In our dealings with the moral imperative here we make particular reference to it characterization in *GNR* and identify the moral imperative in the context of a discussion that isolates the imperative that lies at the basis of all directives of doing, The Law of Objectivity.

In *GNR* we find, especially in the concluding chapter, "The Rational Imperatives," an attempt to get clear on what is morally correct or what is just. That which is right, we find, is that which is done in accord with certain directives of doing, and acting justly is but one of the many modes of correct conduct. Just as there are sets of directives or imperatives, or what Lewis calls *critiques*, governing mental activity or thought, so too are there those for physical doings which fall under the main headings of the technical, the prudential, and the just.[9]

If a factor in ascribing rightness to an action involves its conforming with an imperative, the question arises as to the ground of such an imperative. If this is not spelled out, what is right simply becomes an arbitrary relationship between action and imperative, and the question as to why we can call that right is unanswered. As Lewis puts it, "things are right with respect to a valid principle" and thus we ask "how are they valid, *i.e.*, what is their ground?"[10]

This ground we are looking for is to be distinguished from the "nature" of the right. As to its nature, it is *sui generis*; it is indemonstrable as is any first principle of logic or mathematics.[11] Recognizing just this, of course, would be an unsatisfactory stopping point in the consideration of the right, for it seems that a number of moral systems, like mathematical systems, could be generated from different imperatives or first principles; and there may be no way of choosing among them except that one may be more entrenched in custom than another; as Ayer might point out, we are stubborn and maintain one over the other.[12]

Thus we are interested in not just the nature but the ground of the right. Lewis argues for it summarily in this way. Our nature is such that we must decide. We are thinking and active beings; thought is an essential feature of

4

humans. Thought and thoughtfully determined doing have two characteristics — generality and objectivity. Given that, The Law of Objectivity
becomes the ground of all imperatives of thought and action.

Let us flesh out what is involved with the Law of Objectivity and the
notions of generality and objectivity so that we can clearly understand why
The Law of Objectivity is the ground we are looking for. Generality involves
our bringing with us into new situations our knowledge of the past which we
think relevant to the present situation that we see as similar. Objectivity
leads us to recognize that, because it is only the future we can affect, we must
not simply focus on our *hic et nunc* experiences but project what they will be
in the future given certain present courses of action. We are to apprehend
the future cognitively on the basis of the past.

The command, or Law of Objectivity, whose formulation draws on these
characteristics of thought and ultimately of human nature is stated thus:

> So conduct and determine your activity of
> thinking and doing as to conform any decision
> of them to the objective actualities as cognition
> signifies to you in your representational ap-
> prehension of them and not according to any
> impulsions or solicitations exercised by the
> affective quality of your present experience as
> immediate feeling merely.[13]

To this point, our investigation has led us to the ground of the right but to
no moral imperative or imperative of justice. Lewis' transition depends
upon an observation of human nature, one very much like Hume's[14] and
Mead's,[15] that man is *"imperatively* social,"[16] that it would be misleading to
consider man in some way other than as a being whose development into a
man requires a social context. With this observation about man, Lewis thinks
we can generate the "socially significant counterpart"[17] of the Law of
Objectivity. Lewis does not argue that there is such a counterpart, but I think
that what he has in mind is this. Imperatives direct and determine the
rightness of all our behavior that is corrigible and self-directed. Part of that
behavior involves our interaction with others; we recall that a datum for
ethics is that man is social. This too is governed by an imperative, then. We
can thus expect a restatement of The Law of Objectivity taking into account
the fact that man is a social being. Lewis identifies it as:

> the dictate to govern one's activities affecting

5

other persons as one would if these effects of
them were to be realized with the poignancy of
the immediate — hence in one's own person.[18]

Although we are interested in little more than a brief characterization of
the moral imperative in this section, our dealing with a problem that arises
with the formulation above may help at least to make this brief summary
clearer. The difficulty lies in whether Lewis is simply asking the individual to
consider the effects of his actions on himself in his relations with others
"with the poignancy of the immediate" or whether he is to consider the
effects on his own person in the sense that he is placing himself in another's
shoes. If it were the former, there is no reason to think that we have gotten
any further than The Law of Objectivity. The second alternative suggests
itself and this alternative is supported as the correct one by the observation
that The Law of Moral Equality, which Lewis claims to be a part of the moral
imperative, has us formulate no laws for one that could not be a law for
all.[19] The following reformulation of the moral imperative is needed
then:

... govern one's activities affecting other persons
as one would if these effects of them *on other
persons* were to be realized with the poignancy
of the immediate — hence in one's own person.

These initial considerations of how Lewis deals with justice suggest that
any concern with the moral imperative takes us beyond simply a consideration of justice and to one of right doing generally. Lewis, we saw, was
interested in all modes of right and in their ground. That mode of right,
namely prudence, which at times may be on a collision course with what the
moral demands, is taken up in Chapter 2. There, more specifically, we
consider the question of how we are to deal with the value that can accrue to
a self-interested individual through the satisfaction of his interests. One
dimension of this involves our determining whether the satisfaction of some
interest is in that person's best interests, whether he will be acting *prudently* if
he does satisfy it. It is in this context that we try to get clear on the demands of
prudence and the justification of the prudential imperative. Although we
are highlighting here the individual and his interests, we do not leave
unmentioned how his interests are shaped by his fellow men and how,
when they diverge, the phenomenon can be explained by Lewis' discussion
of idiosyncracies and the distinction he draws between concepts and ideas.
Another dimension is the issue of whether an action done only for one's own

sake can have ethical significance. In this context, we compare prudence and justice on several points.

Chapter 3 involves a general discussion of imperatives which allows us to reconsider an unresolved issue dealt with in the analysis of the prudential imperative — its ground — as well as to formulate remarks general enough to apply to the moral imperative as well. We consider what activity is subject to imperatives, the various modes of imperatives, and their interrelationships. Finally, we offer an analysis of human nature and explore its utility for establishing the ground for the rational directives in a systematic analysis of the various arguments that suggest themselves as candidates.

We pay particular attention in Chapter 4 to society, social value, and the moral imperative, which may be looked at as ordering that value we characterize as social. We consider how Lewis circumvents problems that arise with Kant's formulation of the moral imperative and see how some of the moves involve incorporating utilitarian themes. Lewis' notions of society and social value are then explored with an eye to their relation to the moral imperative.

In the concluding chapter, we identify the components of a naturalistic theory of justice, which best characterizes the outcome of Lewis' attempt to bring together into one ethical theory aspects of Kantianism and utilitarianism. An effort is then made to place Lewis' position in perspective with other ethical theories.

FOOTNOTE REFERENCES FOR CHAPTER 1

[1]C. I. Lewis, "Autobiography," *The Philosophy of C. I. Lewis*, edited by Paul Arthur Schilpp (La Salle: Open Court, 1968), p. 19.

[2]*Ibid.*, p. 21.

[3]*Ibid.*, p. 20.

[4]C. I. Lewis, "The Philosopher Replies," *The Philosophy of C. I. Lewis*, p. 672.

[5]John Lange, "The Late Papers of C. I. Lewis," *Journal of the History of Philosophy*, vol. 14, no. 3, 1966, p. 235.

[6]C. I. Lewis, *The Ground and Nature of the Right* (GNR) New York: Columbia University Press, 1955), pp. 3-5.

[7]Alfred J. Ayer, *Language, Truth, and Logic* (New York: Dover Publications, Inc., 1952), p. 108.

[8]C. I. Lewis, *AKV* (La Salle: Open Court, 1946), p. 553.

[9]Lewis, *GNR,* p. 80.
[10]*Ibid.,* p. 84.
[11]*Ibid.,* p. 83.
[12]Ayer, p. 77.
[13]Lewis, *GNR,* p. 89.
[14]David Hume, *Enquiry Concerning the Principles of Morals, Hume's Moral and Political Philosophy,* p. 190.
[15]George H. Mead, *Mind, Self, and Society,* edited by Charles W. Morris (Chicago: University of Chicago Press, 1934), p. 135.
[16]Lewis, *GNR,* p.90.
[17]Lewis, *GNR,* p. 90.
[18]*Ibid.,* p. 91.
[19]*Ibid.,* pp. 92-93.

CHAPTER 2
INDIVIDUAL INTERESTS & THE DEMANDS OF PRUDENCE

"Well, you tell me; you know as much about it as anybody does."[1] Thus we find Lewis' apparently flippant yet sincere answer to the question, "Why be prudent?" This question should be distinguished from the query of what the prudentially right thing to do is. As we shall see, Lewis never takes us much further than the above answer to the first question with some of his discussion. The second has a more direct and meatier answer and it is with that that we shall begin. I set as our goal in the first part of this chapter a formulation of what it is to act prudently.

After we get a clear understanding of what the imperative of prudence demands, we consider Lewis' attempts to persuade us that there is a critique of prudence and then begin to explore the interrelationships of justice and prudence. We first lay a foundation for the observation that questions of ethics or justice may be thought of as arising when what the individual finds of value differs from what is of public value. Secondly, we make clear that an individual's doing something strictly for his own sake lacks ethical significance and evaluate the claim that no act is so determined by the moral imperative that there is no feature left for prudence to dictate. Finally, we turn from how prudence and justice are demarcated to their affinities.

I

One thing that lies at the foundation of any prudent action is that one takes the future into account by considering what the consequences of his actions have in store for himself, the doer. And in addition, he feels that such behavior is imperative:

> To lack such concern for the future, or feel no imperative to govern one's conduct by reference to it, is to lack a prime requisite of human personality....This first imperative of reason may be regarded as prudential only and directed to the consequences of action for ourselves.[2]

From this we can arrive at a first formulation of a definition that approximates Lewis' meaning of acting prudently. Let us refer to the definitions that we formulate as D_1, D_2, etc., and let us speak of some agent, S, as acting prudently at some particular time t:

9

D_1 *S acts prudently at t* $=$df At *t* having felt constrained to consider, and having considered, the consequences of his act for his life, *S acts accordingly.*

The question that arises over a formulation of this sort is just specifically to what such action is to be directed; what are we looking for in these future consequences? Apropos of this line of questioning, Lewis claims that we are ultimately looking for *a life good on the whole*, borrowing the notion James used to evaluate a life. Put negatively, Lewis claims that "... we may so fail of prudence and thus prejudice some possibility of a good life on the whole...."[3] And further Lewis makes it clear that the pursuit of this end is no less an action that is imperative than what we spoke of in D_1. "Prudence...is its own ultimate kind of right behaving. To be concerned with a life good on the whole is a basic imperative of human nature...."[4] With these new observations I think we can flesh out our initial definition and say:

D_2 *S acts prudently at t* $=$df At *t S* acts to promote a life good on the whole for himself, having felt constrained to consider, and having considered, the consequences of his act for his life in determining how to act.

It is in an explanation of what a life good on the whole consists in that we begin to see the need for revising D_2. At this time we will offer only a rough characterization of the notion but will pay more particular attention to it at the end of this section after we have brought out the essentials of prudent activity. Concerning the notion of a life good on the whole, Lewis claims that it involves "value to one's self in one's whole lifetime with equal consideration of the distant or the nearer eventualities which may be affected by the contemplated act."[5] Lewis also speaks of this as that to which all prudential action is directed.[6] Now if one is to act to maximize the value throughout his life,[7] he is to weigh the various courses of action, one against the other, to see which will bring the most satisfaction. Moreover, the considerations that will weigh into the decision revolve essentially around the consequences of the act:

The rule of prudential action determines what

10

character of actions it is by reason of which the sanction of prudence attaches to them; namely their contributing more to satisfaction in one's whole life than any alternative.[8]

This suggests various emendations to D_2. For one thing, there is nothing in D_2 that keeps one from acting to promote a life good on the whole for himself yet acting imprudently. An obvious example is a case where one's action clearly contributes to his total satisfactions in his lifetime, no dissatisfactions result, yet it was done knowing that there was a course of action that would have yielded greater satisfactions. To avoid calling such a person prudent, even though the action contributed to, and he was acting to promote, a life good on the whole, we offer:

D_3 *S acts prudently at t* =df At t S acts to promote a life good on the whole for himself, having felt constrained to consider, and having considered, the consequences of his act for his life in determining how to act, and in these considerations finding no alternative way of acting that would do more to promote a life good on the whole by increasing total satisfactions.

If this definition has any shortcomings, it is because of its failing to bring out clearly that, while acting prudently involves a factual determination of the consequences of alternatives open to us, we are speaking of "future fact," and we must, in order to reach the decision, predict.[9]

Taking this into account, Lewis is forced to answer the following question with a "no:"

whether we shall be speaking judiciously if we say that a decision of prudential action and the act decided on be objectively right just in case it is true that this action will contribute more of value to the doer's good life than any alternative open to him.[10]

His answer, of course, is based on our above observations concerning the role of prediction in acting prudently. We cannot say at time t that it is *true*

11

that certain values will *in fact* come to the doer as consequences of his act. For if we did, we would be committed to holding that no one can ever act prudently, as such action then becomes predicated on as yet unestablished powers of pre-cognition. What we can achieve in our actions, says Lewis, has no guarantee of truth but only a warrant of probability.[11] In an attempt to capture these insights, D_3 is revised to become:

D_4 *S acts prudently at t* =df At t S acts to promote a life good on the whole for himself, having felt constrained to consider, and having considered, the consequences of his act for his life in determining how to act, and in these considerations finding no alternative way of acting that might more likely promote a life good on the whole by increasing total satisfactions.

Now, we will get different answers to the question of whether an act is prudentially right, depending upon whether we are judging from the critique of subjective or objective rightness. What I would like to do is indicate how this distinction relates to D_4 but does not require our revising it. According to Lewis:

the point of the difference between objective rightness and subjective rightness is, thus, that an act is subjectively right if it conforms to the doer's conviction concerning what consequences are likely to follow and their having that character which marks them as justified to bring about. But an act is objectively right only if this conviction is a cognitively correct judgment — a probability-conclusion correctly drawn from the available evidence.[12]

Based on this and D_4 I think we can say that S acts with subjective prudential rightness at t just in case S acts prudently at t and S is convinced that his assessment of the situation is correct. Accordingly, we say that S acts with objective prudential rightness at t just in case S acts prudently at t and S is cognitively correct in his judgment.

12

Another thing that might be noted about D_4 is that it can be expressed more concisely using some of Lewis' technical terms, especially his notion of contributory value. In *AKV* we find contributory value defined quite simply as having "a potentiality for contributing a value-quality to experience."[13] Now it is the case that the value-quality Lewis is speaking of here involves those satisfactions mentioned in D_4, what is immediately valuable. And our assessment of that which has contributory value presupposes our recognition of the immediately valuable. Both, then, will be involved in acting prudently, for we are interested in value contributing to a life good on the whole, in maximizing total satisfactions or what is immediately valuable:

> . . . there are modes of valuation corresponding to modes of the imperative. Value as contributory. . .and the rational imperative to subordinate, as ends of action, the values findable in transient experience to the goodness of a life to be found good on the whole may serve as illustration.[14]

Employing the notion of contributory value, we can restate D_4 as:

> D_4. *S acts prudently at t* =df At *t S* acts to promote the value maximally contributing to a life good on the whole for himself.

One may object here that this does not capture all of D_4, as it makes no mention of acting in accord with a feeling of constraint to consider the future. But what I wish to contend is that when one is acting to promote contributory value, he is already committed to considering the future, and it seems that, for Lewis, such activity that is not the result of responding to immediate inclinations involves some degree of constraint. And this approximation of acting prudently is not so far from what Lewis says about prudence in one of his latest lectures published in 1959:

> The definitive nature of prudence — our concept of prudence — is exhibited and delineated by the maxim of prudence: So act as to maximize your possible realizations of the good, as against the bad, in your life as a whole.[15]

Here, although contributory value is not mentioned, it is clear that Lewis is trying to set out the essential elements of prudence and feels that it is not necessary to mention constraint when one is considering the future or when one is being told to do so.

Let us now look more carefully at the notion of a life good on the whole. Any detailed characterization of the notion of a life good on the whole is admittedly lacking in Lewis' writings. This is not to indicate that Lewis' basic intuition is unclear, but I propose spelling out clearly what is involved with this idea and doing so by drawing heavily upon some spadework done by John Rawls on an essentially related topic, that of rational life plans. Indeed, Rawls agrees that the intuitive idea "is quite straightforward but unfortunately setting out the details is somewhat tedious."[16] We will first bring out why this material of Rawls is relevant here. This will be followed by an exposition and critique of those thoughts and finally an attempt to assimilate what we can accept of Rawls' views with our definition of prudence.

If there is to be any useful comparison drawn between Lewis and Rawls, a fundamental thing to establish is that one acts to promote a life good on the whole just in case he acts in accord with a rational life plan. Let me try to make this plausible. It is clear that, for Lewis, one is not concerned with maximizing satisfactions in a lifetime simply in the sense of producing as many satisfying experiences as possible. For we have agreed that it is the prudential imperative that advises which satisfying experiences are to be sought; we would thus not expect satisfactions that may accrue from imprudent behavior to constitute a contribution to our effort to create a life good on the whole. Now if the goal is to maximize satisfactions, and if it is assumed that this can be done, then, I suppose that we can attribute to the actor an understanding of his wants and what he is to do to provide for them. And once a person is described in such a way, we can say that he has a plan for action. We have characterized prudent activity as rational and furthermore as taking into account a person's whole life; there is then some sense to our biconditional above that relates a life good on the whole to a pre-analytic understanding of a rational life plan.

Before detailing Rawls' specific views concerning rational life plans, I think it important to point to some incongruities between Rawls' and Lewis' positions when placed in the larger scope of their enterprises. Rawls uses the notion of a rational life plan in working out his view that what is good for some person is that which is right for him to acquire with reference to his rational life plan. Lewis, on the other hand, has the right ordering various individual goods which are established to be such independently of any consideration of right. But in both cases acting in accord with a rational life plan is involved.

The pertinent information from Rawls that we will want to consider can be divided into three main categories — a characterization of long-term plans, the principles of choice of plans, and a reconsideration of long-term plans in the light of the principles of choice. Some of the more important features of long-term plans include: (1) the distant future is less clearly mapped out than the near; (2) the degree of specificity of the plan is proportional to one's knowledge and the understanding of his interests; (3) rather than consisting of a blueprint of action for one's life, the long-term plan is essentially a set of sub-plans. One ranks the importance of the satisfaction of the various desires according to their generality and orders the sub-plans accordingly.[17]

There are six principles associated with the choice of a rational life plan, the first three included under Rawls' "principles of rational choice;" the latter, under "time-related principles". The first group includes the principle of inclusiveness, which directs us to choose one plan over another on the ground that one fosters and fulfills all the goals of the other in addition to at least one more. Another principle in this group directs the rational man to prefer the plan that is most effective in obtaining the goal, but the goal is qualified according to the principle of inclusiveness which has us prefer those plans that encourage the satisfactions of wider or more varied interests. The third principle, the principle of greater likelihood, supports, according to Rawls, the directions of the second. It simply has us prefer the plan that is more likely to be executed, *ceteris paribus*.[18]

Of the time-related principles, the principle of postponement has us search for the rational plan that gives us sufficient time to obtain the relevant facts before prematurely binding us to a course of action. Another has us prefer plans that provide for expectations that rise over the years (or at least do not decline) to those without such provisions. The third principle (of continuity) has these features:

> It reminds us that since a plan is a scheduled
> sequence of activities, earlier and later activities
> are bound to affect one another. The whole plan
> has a certain unity, a dominant theme. There is
> not, so to speak, a separate utility function for
> each period.[19]

Let us now look more closely at the rational life plan in the light of what we have said about the principles of choice. Rawls further characterizes his

15

notion of the rational plan (we assume this applies to rational life plans) by saying that it is that plan that one with deliberative rationality chooses. He claims to be drawing on Sidgwick's notion of "a person's future good on the whole."[20] He goes on to describe the plan chosen with deliberative rationality as "the plan that would be dicided upon as the outcome of careful reflection in which the agent reviewed, in the light of all relevant facts, what it would be like to carry out these plans and thereby ascertain the course of action that would best realize his more fundamental desires."[21]

Throughout, it is clear that Rawls is mentioning *the* plan, but how strictly are we to interpret this? Of course, if he simply means the plan that is chosen from the competing plans at any particular time, there is no problem. But from other comments of his, it becomes clearer that once the plan is chosen, it is not contemplated that a different life-plan will replace it: "Now one feature of a rational plan is that in carrying it out the individual does not change his mind and wish that he had done something else instead."[22] Further, I think the last time-related principle we mentioned above supports this interpretation. We find Rawls cognizant of the fact that the past colors the future and, too, that the future (and presumably the present) influences our perception of the past. Yet we further observe that, on Rawls' view, the principle only *reminds* us of this. We are given no directive concerning the choice of life plans as we are with the other plans. Rawls presents the content of the principle as simply something we are to keep in mind as we work out our life plan; there is no provision for the present and future coloring the past such that we may want to adopt a different life plan — the principle offers no guidance for handling such a situation, should it arise.

While it is not important to pin such a view on Rawls, I do think it of significance to work out an acceptable and clear position concerning the adoption of different life plans throughout one's life and the bearing that present, past, and future experiences may have on this. I would like to draw a distinction that I think may make our reading of Rawls plausible in addition to allowing for a change in life plans. Basically, what I would like to suggest is that while the initial choice of the rational life plan may be rational, one can conceivably shift from one life plan to another, perhaps unwittingly, by means other than those that initially led him to choose the first; and this means referred to essentially involves the continuity of satisfactions mentioned earlier.

Let me make this clearer. The point is that the interrelation of present, past, and future satisfactions may allow for the transition from one life plan to another, perhaps without the individual's ever rationally deciding to make such a switch. Novel present satisfactions, to begin at an arbitrary starting point, may influence how we view our past satisfactions as well as our future. And the new view of the past may reinforce our desire for such in the future. As we move into the future with such an attitude, those novel satisfactions that occurred in the present are now part of the past, allowing for a new basis with which to view the present. And so on. We might abstract from this the view that indeed there is much continuity in our experiences but not simply a linear continuity with the past influencing the present and the future, but a more dynamic one, as brought out above, that could conceivably lead one to pass from one long range life plan to another, without, perhaps, making a rational choice to do so.

An example may be helpful. Consider an undergraduate who at time t has a life plan arrived at with deliberative rationality. He sees his ultimate objective as being financially well off, having a prestigious role in the community, and being able to maintain both in life with a minimal chance of losing them, *i.e.*, he wants an occupation that basically guarantees that he will have these as a matter of course. His plan is to become a medical doctor and he is well on his way, let us say, in his freshman year.

One evening he attends a piano recital which makes him very nostalgic of past performances of his own and of music generally. He decides that he has been neglecting music to foster other important interests while at school and schedules a music theory course and resumes his lessons during the next semester. More formally we might see his attending the concert as an event in the present that brought into focus and colored favorably various satisfactions of the past. And both have influenced his expectations of future satisfactions.

The further development of our example, I'm sure, is becoming clear. One music course leads to another and he majors in music while still maintaining his status as a pre-medical student by taking the minimally required courses. He also becomes involved in giving performances at various campuses; he publishes an article in music theory. His former, main objectives are less important to him now and excellence in performance and scholarly work has become an end in itself. Further, it happens that the time the medical school entrance examination is being administered conflicts with a performance, and he performs instead of taking the examination. He is encouraged by professors to pursue graduate studies in music and does so, his other main objectives going more by the wayside than his deciding at

17

any one point to put them there.

During his graduate studies, he is exposed to others who are living lives of the sort towards which he is now directed; he begins to construct a rational plan for life based on what he knows now about his situation and the possibilites open to him. His former life plan is no longer a live option. He has passed into a new situation where he is prepared to make a rational choice of a new life plan, although he has never formally decided to replace his former life plan with a new one.

On the one hand we have allowed for one's changing his life plan but have also made room for Rawls' position that one does not at any one point decisively change his mind in mid-course about the plan, that he does not regret not having adopted a different plan, and that he does not dread the consequences of the plan he is following.[23] I propose that with these qualifications of Rawls' views, we accept them as providing a detailed characterization of Lewis' notion of a life good on the whole and thus ultimately in assisting us to understand Lewis' notion of acting prudently.

II

We are now prepared to direct our attention briefly to some comments of Lewis' on the question of why be prudent and to his thought on deriving or justifying a prudential imperative or giving reasons for acting prudently, all of which he seems to deal with as the same problem. We follow up on what we observed earlier, that acting prudently is imperative. And if the reader recalls, that is basically all that we did do earlier — observe that that was the case. This was not being unfaithful to the text of *AKV*, for Lewis points out there that the prudential imperative "requires no reason; being itself the expression of that which is the root of all reason; that in the absence of which there would be no reason of any sort for anything."[24]

I suspect that from this statement it is fair to conclude that acting prudently is not outside the sphere of the rational in that it is the root of all reason. In a sense, if one wanted a reason for acting prudently, it seems that another might offer that a philosophy that called for acting imprudently would be totally nihilistic and would not allow us to be reasonable in an area (philosophy) where we have that as our aim. And he might go on to argue that because of the undesirable consequences of not acting prudently, it, is imperative to act prudently. Although Lewis holds that acting prudently needs no reason, what he claims after that could be construed as an offering, in part, of an explanation of why we are to act prudently.

It is questionable, however, how one seriously offering such an argument could expect it to convince one toward whom it is to be directed, *viz.,* one who wants a reason to act prudently. Presumably he would be irrational and there is no reason to suspect that reason could convince such a person. Furthermore it is true that acting prudently for Lewis is rational, where acting rationally is acting in accord with imperatives and acting prudently is imperative. If one asks, therefore, for a rationale for prudence, he ultimately asks for one for being rational, and as Peirce put it, "one cannot well demand a reason for reasonableness itself."[25] In effect, one cannot well give a reason for reasonableness itself. Basically, I think that this type of reasoning is operative in the following passage in *GNR* where it is clear that Lewis is not concerned with deriving or justifying the prudential imperative, but rather assuming throughout that there is one, at least when he speaks of acting prudently as being rational:

> Also, if few acts are without effect upon others so that there may be none which will be wholly exempt from the critique of moral justice, it is likewise true that there are none at all which are without effect upon the doer himself and are exempt from critical examination from the point of view of prudence. Prudential concern for one's own interest certainly is rational, and its projected end, like the goodness of others for which we are morally concerned, is something which will not take care of itself without attention but perennially calls for critical consideration of our contemplated acts The modes of criticism of doing as right and wrong are, thus, various.[26]

My point can be made even clearer, I think, by showing how an unpacking of "rational" in the above quotation leads us to an understanding that prudence is imperative. I construct the argument in this way. From the agent's point of view, none of his acts are without effects upon himself and his interests. Prudential concern ranges over all the acts of an individual. Prudential concern is rational. Rational activity involves activity that is subject to critique involving imperatives to act in certain ways. Thus it is imperative to act prudently. This it should be made clear is an observation concerning the "rationality" of prudence, that the rational man is constrained to look out for his own interests.

19

While Lewis affirms in some passages of *GNR* his position taken in *AKV*, that we cannot give a reason for acting prudently, in other passages it may seem that we can. Consider the following:

> And if it not be granted without argument that the prudential assessment is a required mode of judgment, then it should be sufficient to point out that none of us could well determine what justice dictates unless we be able to weigh the interests of others — their self-interest. Conversely, if the doer's own interest be not already included in what just action must depend upon, the just man could hardly have any ground for judging the interest of others if he lacked the capacity to judge his own. If it does not go without saying that one ought to be prudent ... then it should require no more than the question why we are so concerned to inculcate prudence as well as justice in our children, to assure the point that prudence is some kind of dictate ...and has some manner of its own validity.[27]

There seem to be two lines of arguing here for acting prudently, but both, I think, upon inspection, do not amount to giving reasons for being prudent or in deriving a prudential imperative. In the second argument that begins with "if it does not go without saying. . .," Lewis clearly is merely arguing to show why it should go without saying; he draws attention to certain things that in fact we do and indicates that the prudential imperative and our recognition of it is tacit or implicit in our behavior. As for the first argument, I think the two key propositions can be formulated thus:

> (1) If we can well determine what justice dictates, then we can weigh the interests of others.
>
> (2) If we can weigh the interest of others, then we must be able to weigh (judge) our own interests.

The only way it seems that one can plausibly derive the conclusion or consequent of (2) is to affirm the antecedent of (1), which then allows him to affirm the antecedent of (2) and thus get the consequent of (2). But even if we allow him to affirm (1)'s antecedent, the most he is able to prove is that we must be able to weigh (judge) our own interests which is not the same as what the prudential imperative we defined earlier demands of us.

To this point we have seen that in *GNR* not much headway can be made in deriving a prudential imperative. Although it is not of particular importance whether Lewis intended these arguments to be defeasible, it seems likely that he was aware of their weaknesses, as each one is prefaced by a phrase indicating that no reasons need to be given for the prudential imperative. We find that in the cases where we first thought we may have had reasons for positing a prudential imperative, they fail to provide us with any good argument.

It is at the end of *GNR* that we find that much of what we have discussed in this section has been along the right lines, that, in fact, no derivation of the prudential imperative is possible:

> If there are any first principles of right, or first principles of the various categories of the right — and it is, of course, such first or most comprehensive principles which we should seek — it lies in the nature of the case that the validity of them will be indemonstrable.[28]

This much explains why no derivation of the prudential imperative is possible; and furthermore, two paragraphs after the above quotation, Lewis points to what happens when reasons for the prudential imperative are given: "Any attempt to induce recognition of principles of right as valid, can only appeal to some antecedent sense of such rightness which will, at some point, constrain any reasonable person to acknowledge them."[29] I do not think this is far from our earlier observation that prudence and rationality are intimately related in that part of acting rationally included acting prudently. Moreover, that we find no derivation of the prudential imperative is not surprising in that we find one for no imperative. But as we observed earlier, we can still inquire into the ground of these imperatives, the prudential included, recalling that "the ground of validity of imperatives must somehow lie in our human nature,"[30] in addition to there being the pragmatic self-contradiction involved in denying them. These matters we will attend to in some detail in the next chapter.

III

To this point we have concerned ourselves with how prudence prescribes individual valuings to be ordered as well as with the question of whether some justification for the prudential imperative might be offered.

21

In this section we continue to focus on individual valuings and, in particular, how they make inroads into our considerations of justice.

Now, in *AKV*, Lewis suggests that if what some individual found of value never differed from what others desired and found of value. (One might imagine, along with Mill, that it has become second nature for all in the society to think only in terms of public utility[31]), distinctively ethical considerations may never arise: "And unless what is genuinely valuable to the individual should be different on occasion from what has value to the public, no contrariety between egoism and impartial consideration of all would be discernable, and this ethical problem would have no meaning."[32] And there is the suggestion that it is only infrequently that such individual valuings occur. The question arises as to what the conceptual underpinnings are of these individual valuings which may be of no public value but which seem essential if ethical questions are to arise.

Passages in *MWO*, where Lewis deals with the distinction between ideas and concepts, are relevant in giving a genetic account of the occurrence of the peculiar individual valuings we spoke of. A consideration of these passages is important to show that the occurrence of such valuings is part of a more general theory concerning social cooperation and that they are not striking discontinuities in a philosophy that is establishing a tight fit between the individual and his social order.

Most generally, Lewis shows in *MWO* how it is that we have a common world; his comments on the individual apropos of our present considerations are a by-product of this analysis. It is because we have a common conceptual framework (the *a priori* which arose from our common needs to control the environment)[33] that we can, in large, act as a social unit. Now if the realm of the *a priori* determines in part how we will interpret immediately given experience, and given a common stock of meanings among members of the society, then the members of the community will see things with a common eye. Any expression of individual interests or idiosyncracies will be the result of that individual's recognizing that he is deviating from the norm and defining his interests. Now this is rare, as individual thought itself proceeds along the lines of common meanings and usually any individual distinctions are suppressed.[34]

Even if such an expression is forthcoming, it is doubtful that it will have any socially significant impact upon the behavior of members in the society, as they have no concept with which to make this distinction. This does not mean that such idiosyncracies cannot influence others in the society and cause them eventually to create new concepts to handle what they now see to be an important distinction. But then if others do see it as such, and a concept is created to handle it, this means that no longer is some peculiar individual interest involved, but rather one of the other members of the society, and thus the situation that we are interested in concerning the deviation of some individual's interest is no longer. We are therefore interested in the case where the distinction is one that will not have any such impact on society; and as we already observed, that is rare:

> If these distinctions which only some can make directly in the context of their experience, do not concern what is important for behavior adjustment, then very likely no socially current concept will be framed in terms of them. There will be no language to describe these personal and peculiar phases of experience. And — remembering how largely our thought is informed by social relationships — it is likely that these phases of experience will largely pass unnoticed by the individual himself.[35]

To this point, Lewis has said little to evaluate the worth of these idiosyncrasies, given that they do crop up. There is one passage in *MWO*, however, that seems to cast their significance for the individual or for society in a negative light. And if this is so, one might conclude that they *should* be suppressed. But this is an odd conclusion given Lewis' characterization of peculiar individual valuings in *AKV*. We will, then, want to look at these claims more closely.

We saw above how these idiosyncrasies are tied in with communication — society will probably ignore them, as it has no concepts with which to speak of them let alone to recognize them, and the concepts of society usually suppress even the individual's idiosyncratic tendencies from coming to the surface of his consciousness. Lewis tells us concerning communication that its "eventual aim" is "the coordination of behavior".[36] Now if the aim is *coordination* of behavior and idiosyncrasies are by definition deviations from the generally coordinated behavior of the members of a society, then one way to promote the realization of this aim is to suppress idiosyncrasies.

This type of a conclusion based on our drawing out the implications of the proposition stating the aim of communication is not far off the track in interpreting Lewis' views; indeed Lewis points out that our ostensive behavior is what is important in coordinated activity and not what we individually feel. He thus suggests that even if we feel differently, act the same:

> My words must maintain a certain relation to other words which I use and to the things I do. It is necessary that we should act alike, in fundamental and important ways, if we are to have a possible basis for understanding one another. But it is *not* necessary that when we act alike we should *feel* alike, however large the presumption that actually we do.[37]

Lewis does not qualify his position here and because of that there is nothing that would stop us from applying this analysis to the concept of red or, just as easily, to the concept of good. Regardless of how we feel, whatever our idiosyncracies may be, we can and should act to promote a coordinated community.

Let us go on now to see how Lewis qualifies the conclusions we arrived at. He does this in "Appendix C" of *MWO*, basically by drawing a distinction between ideas and concepts.[38] Lewis here deals with the difference between my meaning of good and my meaning of red. If I immediately apprehend something differently than others do when they apply the concept of red, but yet I apply the concept as they do, "then my cognitive *concept* of red would be identical with that of other persons, regardless of its peculiar quality as immediately given."[39]

There is no objection, then, to dealing with "red" as suggested by the foregoing analysis. However, we cannot deal with "good" in the same way, says Lewis, thus qualifying the conclusion we reached above:

> But if my meaning of the 'good' should represent a similar idiosyncracy then the purposes for the sake of which I have framed and use this term would be defeated, whether I should know it or not. I do not *mean* to designate as 'good' what other persons merely behave toward in the same way I do or find in the same contexts as I do: I intend by it that which affects them with the same, or similar, qualities of experience with which I am affected in the presence of it.

24

> Notions so framed may appropriately be termed
> 'ideas'. Such ideas are basic for the
> science of values; for ethics, aesthetics, and the
> philosophy of religion.[40]

While we may have no objection to designating as red what other persons merely *behave* toward in the same way I do or find in the same contexts as I do, this cannot be done with good. For part of what I mean by it is a certain intersubjectivity of given experience, and any meaning of it that did not take this into account would be confused. The Kantian distinction between concepts or categories and ideas, a distinction Lewis is heavily relying on in the above quotation but one which is not spelled out at all, is helpful in understanding Lewis' view here.

For Kant, ideas are ideals for which the human mind strives, major ones including unity of self and of the world. They guide our activity and represent an upper limit we can only approximate. Concepts, on the other hand, are constitutive and not regulative like ideas. They allow us to organize what is presented to us in intuition, much as concepts handle Lewis' given.[41] I think that the main or essential feature of ideals that Lewis is drawing on for his distinction is that one must in some way identify with the ideal, he must actually be *guided* by the ideal if we are correctly describing his activity as goal oriented. With ideals, the focus is on the individual and his relation to them, not on some outward display of behavior where we can only guess whether the individual is being influenced by the ideal. Accordingly, Lewis demands of the idea of good, unlike the concept of red, that it bear a like relation to each person using it, that what I *experience* when I use "good" be the same or very similar to what others experience when they employ "good."

With this distinction, as we suggested above, Lewis is able to avoid the undesirable conclusions that one is to act as if he were experiencing satisfactions as others do whenever he used "good" even if he was not having such experiences. In the problematic passage above Lewis was dealing only with concepts and feelings associated with them, and thus it needed to be qualified by introducing the notion of ideas which are incommensurable with concepts and have a logic of their own.

What I would now like to argue is that Lewis' treatment of the individual and the idea of good lies at the foundation, in some sense, of an individual's interests differing, on occasion, from what is of public value. It is not the case that those who sense differently from others, when they employ the concept red in their experience, splinter off from others in society and speak of their interests apart from those of others in society. Nor does society recognize such individuals as having any peculiar interests. And Lewis recognized this when he pointed out that those whose experience of red is different from that of others should (and probably do, in fact) conform to society's use of the predicate in the interests of communication. One usually does not speak of *his* red; such idiosyncracies are suppressed.

On the other hand, we have the peculiar situation, when it comes to goods, of individuals' claiming certain things as good only for themselves and recognizing other goods as primarily public. Now, if Lewis held that the idea of good functioned as the concept of red, he could not account for this difference. But in dealing with good in a way where individual feelings or sensings are paramount, he can account for one's contrasting his own good with the public good. It is Lewis' treatment of the idea of good, then, that provides the groundwork for situations of peculiar individual valuings we encountered in *AKV*, and which ultimately are the source, as we saw, of an ethical problem arising.

IV

Explaining why no action done strictly with regard to self-interest is just will set us up nicely for a consideration of the degree to which prudential concerns may enter into one's action once the moral dictate has made its claim. We find in *GNR* that one reason why no strictly self-interested action is just is because of the way we delimit our subject matter and define what is just. Ethics deals with what is just and what is just involves a consideration of the interests of others. This is not to say that the prudential concern is not an important consideration for ethics. Indeed, a discussion of what is just for Lewis, as we shall see, calls for a consideration of individual self-interest as well as the interests of others. In other words, although a consideration of self-interest is a component in determining what is just, it is not the only one. Thus it makes sense to claim that no strictly prudential action is just and at the same time to hold that an important consideration of justice involves individual self-interest. In the following passage, where Lewis has not yet defined the just, we can see his pre-analytic reasoning on delimiting the subject matter:

> The question of the relation between prudence
> and justice is an inevitable topic of ethics; and
> the questions of prudent behavior, apart from
> or beyond the questions of justice, constitute an

inevitable problem of human life. Whether questions of the prudentially sanctioned as such are moral issues, would seem to depend mainly upon how one chooses to delimit application of the term, 'moral'. To exclude them from ethics is possibly justified in the interest of the seperation of problems. That however seems dubious: one could also think that such exclusion masks a derogation of the actual importance of prudential behavior or betokens an overweening inclination to the edifying. In any case, the prudential questions are problems of right conductand, if excluded from ethics, must find their place in the larger topic of practical philosophy (or philosophy of practice) concerned with principles of our rational self-government of action.[42]

Once Lewis does in fact begin unpacking the notion of justice, its immediate relationship to prudence becomes clear; from there Lewis goes on to refine this formulation. I think his reasoning can be stated as follows. Justice decrees that the interests of all are to be considered equally whenever one acts. Thus the doer's own interests are to be considered (for one). Now, prudential concerns can be overruled in the interest of justice. Furthermore there is always some feature of every act that is not determined by what is just. Moreover, the prudential imperative is categorical. Thus, some feature of every act is governed by prudential concerns.[43] And, *a fortiori*, some feature of an act dictated by justice is governed by prudential concerns.

Each of these statements can be considered seperately in the light of the supporting arguements in their favor. Let us consider the first statement from
from the argument, that justice decrees that the interest of all are to be considered equally. At this point no argument is presented for this and we assume it is either to be taken on face value or as definitional. Indeed, it appears in a conditional the antecedent of which, for Lewis' point to be made, is clearly affirmed, indicating that such a proposition is to be taken simply as being the case at this time. (The conditional I speak of is "If justice requires giving weight to the interest of another equally as to one's own, that

equation is also reversible. . . .)[44]

If Lewis is, for the time, assuming the truth of the first proposition, let us for the moment accept it and examine the second, that the doer's own interests are to be considered. This of course follows immediately from the first and to be sure, Lewis point out that "justice presupposes the validity of the prudential aim."[45] The third proposition in the argument under consideration, that justice can overrule prudential aims, is simply stated by Lewis and is never given a much deeper treatment, as it is assumed that among the featrures of the critique of justice is that it takes precedence over prudence. It is wrong-headed to reason that if one's interest (that count for one) are outnumbered, in considering the interests of all, as the critique of justice demands, then the prudential concerns of the individual are outvoted, overruled, as it were, and justice has run its course. For such reasoning would be tantamount to saying that the interests of society prevail in a conflict with an individual and in that justice is done. But we recall that that is where the question of justice begins.

We are thus led to a consideration of the last two statements (excluding the conclusion), the first being that there is always some feature of every act that is not determined by justice. In support of this Lewis says:

> I ought to pay my bill and satisfy my creditor;
> but payment by check or cash, today or on the
> first of next month, may satisfy his just claim,
> and allow me justly to determine these alterna-
> tives by reference to any prudential considera-
> tion which may affect them. It lies in the fact that
> what any directive of action will dictate is only a
> way of acting, and not some utterly specific
> doing. . . .[46]

This claim of Lewis' about prudence and justice is part of his more comprehensive view that no rule that completely determines the future act in every respect is one that is fit for humans. And this is part of Lewis' analysis of human nature which we will wxamine in more detail later. Let us here at least mention that if we can agree that essential features of human nature included acting according to rules and being able to choose, then we suspect that any rule designed to rule out choice is a rule that is not designed for humans.

This brings us then to the final statement, that the prudential imperative is categorical. In *GNR* Lewis is arguing for this only in a certain sense:

Since any hypothetical directive becomes categorical when the 'if' of it is satisfied, the prudential directives, whose 'if' is that of wanting to be happy, have a force of 'always' rather than of 'when'. In that sense, the prudential imperative is categorical rather than hypothetical.[47]

It is clear at this point that from this unpacking of a categorical imperative, we are not able to pass to the conclusion with any ease. The fact that the prudential imperative is categorical does not itself mean that it always has some application, even if some features of an act are not determined by justice. While it may be true that we always want to be happy, it seems there may be occasions when there is no specific directive applicable to the situation that could suggest how one might contribute to his happiness, even though the demands of justice have not determined the entire act. What we find, then, is that there is a suppressed assumption that everything one does can be advised in some way by prudence, and this, in fact, has been asserted earlier in *GNR* by Lewis:

there are none (a doer's acts, my insertion) at all which are without effect upon the doer himself and are exempt from critical examination from the point of view of prudence. Prudential concern for one's interest certainly is rational.[48]

With this claim, there seems to be no difficulty in arriving at the conclusion. But this additional premise does seem to be a rather sweeping generalization open to counter-examples that are not only damaging to it but to the whole argument.

A situation is conceivable where one has no interests about a certain act after the dictate of justice has overruled the original prudential interest on the matter. Consider the situation where one is directed, in the interests of justice, to die for the state or society. Of course it is conceivable that he may have certain remaining interests as to how this will come about. We recall that Anne Boleyn preferred beheading to burning; that no doubt she chose to go submissively but nobly rather than being dragged and screaming along the way.

Yet it is just as conceivable in such a situation that one be plunged into the depths of despair, as it were, and have no interest in the matter at all. And this is all a result of justice's overriding his prudential interest in life. While justice's dictate did not *logically* determine the entire act ot dying for the state and allowed for the possibility of there being room for the prudential imperative to operate, it did, at least in the case above, *practically* determine the situation such that there is no remaining self-interest that could be directed by prudential critique. If this much can be accepted, then it the conclusion to the argument under consdieration is dubious.

The criticism may continue along the lines that Lewis seems to be capitalizing on a shakey distinction between an act and the features of an act. Why should Anne Boleyn's act of dying for the state include the feature of her going submissively to the platform where the swordsman is? Certainly these are not identical actions so why *cannot* they be treated as individual acts? It seems that when one begins to speak of the features of an act as Lewis does, one could extend the notion of act to take in so large a segment of physical activity that eventually something will fall under the prudential critique. But as we saw, counter-examples can be offered if the "act" does not grow to uncontrollable dimensions.

In bring out precisely what *is* wrong with the main counter-examples under consideration, I think we can come to a better understanding of Lewis' position. First, it is clear that the moral imperative or the demands of justice could ever require the taking of a life. The example at hand is equivocating on justice for it deals with the justice of some civil society. Secondly, even if we allow that, *per absurdum,* the moral law directs one's death, the effects of this on the condemned, as stated in the counter-instance, does not seriously cut into Lewis' claim that justice does not completely determine the act. Again, Lewis is mainly concerned to argue that the moral law is an appropriate directive, in that there is nothing in the law itself that rules out some features of choice on how aspects of the as yet undetermined future are to be dealt with. Thus, the moral law has not in the revelant sense completely determined the situation. Thirdly, even if the second point here is accepted, the proponent of the counter-example may still claim to have provided a situation where there is no function for the critique of prudence. And to this we can answer that even if there is in fact nothing for prudence to determine in the situation, what of it? Lewis' claim, for one thing, is about acts (and their consequences) of a doer and not about some state of affairs the doer is in. Also, we find in Chapter 3 that it is activity that is decisionable, self-governed, corrigible, and deliberable that is subjected to critique. It is very doubtful whether any of the person's behavior described in the counter-example could fit this description.

Finally, Lewis need not be troubled by the criticism concerning the features of an act; for it is an act and its predictable consequences that the critique of prudence evaluates. So Lewis cannot be said to be stretching the notion of an act simply to let prudential concerns enter in, for it is more that the bare act that the critique evaluates in the first place. We thus find that the proposed counter-example does little to shake the argument that establishes that some feature of an act dictated by justice is governed by prudential concerns.

V

There are further ways in which prudence and justice are related, Lewis offers a genetic account of one's development into a just man holding, basically, that one can take others into account and act justly towards them only if their interests can be understood; and that requires one's being able to deal with his own interests intelligently. This statement of the psychological hypothesis involved is admittedly vague, but then Lewis' formulation of it is confusing at times. I hope to get clear on where he does stand and then critically evaluate that view.

The point Lewis is trying to make, I think, is a familiar one and is implicit in a comment like "How can you be a marriage counsellor if you've never been married?" Lewis' explication of this sometimes takes the form of contrasting respect for our own future interests with the present interest of others;[49] sometimes of prudence with justice;[50] sometimes of a mixture of prudence and self-interests with justice and the interest of others.[51] And throughout these passages we find mentioned the *validity* of prudential aims and of the interests of others, *respect* for interests, and a *capacity* for acting prudently. Questions inevitably arise as to how one can put these factors together, whether one can, *e.g.*, act justly given a capacity for prudent activity, a disregard for his self-interests, and a sensitivity or respect for the interests of others.

In order to deal with such a question or similar ones where the various terms and contrasts of Lewis' terminology are mixed and it is unclear whether any category boundaries have been crossed or whether any answer, however plausible, is correct, I think we should sharpen up these contrasts and get clear on where these concepts are demarcated, stayin as close to Lewis' work as possible. There are a number of variables to consider. First of all, I suggest, in accord with our earlier discussion of what it is to act prudently, that distinctions be drawn among whether or not one acts prudently, whether he knows what the prudent thing to do is (and is thus capable of acting in such a manner) whether he acts with regard to his self-interests (and thus respects them), and whether he knows what is in his self-interest. Parallel distinctions can be drawn among whether or not one acts justly, whether he knows what the just thing to do is, whether he acts with regard for the interests of others, and whether he knows what is in the interests of others.

Now knowing what the prudent thing to do is and acting prudently are sub-divisions of acting in accord with one's self-interests and knowing what is in one's self-interest, respectively. Furthermore, one cannot act prudently unless he knows what it is prudent to do, for, as we observed earlier, acting prudently is a technical term involving imperative constaint attaching to knowledge of the situation. Similarly, one cannot act justly unless he knows what the just thing to do is. And acting justly and knowing what the just thing to do is are sub-divisions of acting with regard for the interests of others and knowing what the interest of others are, respectively.

Now it should be noted that Lewis introduces the dimension of prudence and self-interests to the discussion of justice when he tries to answer the question of how we can know of the interests of others and why we should respect them. Taking this into account, and bringing with us the understanding we reached of the concepts discussed above, it seems the appropriate question to ask is whether we can know what the interests of others are such that we can act justly without having had parrallel experiences or without having dealt with the interests involved prudently? Once the question is stated along the lines of Lewis' intent for bringing in prudence and self-interest, I think the answer now becomes more clearly yes. We may have had no experience paralleling the sacrificing of Iphigenia nor any interest paralleling her contemporaries with respect to that situation, yet we can still apprehend what their interests were, and, given that we were time travelers and journeyed to that society, we suppose that we could act justly towards them. The significant parallel between self-interests and others' interests is that I do not have to *experience* the interests of others to deal with them any more than I must actually experience my future interests in order to deal with them.

What we have done is to have found what the significant and fundamental form of the question was that Lewis was asking. And that involved our sorting out the interrelationships of the several concepts under consideration as well as determining just why Lewis thought self-interests played an important role in acting justly. Now one may still be interested in further psychological questions of whether I could grasp another's account of his interests without an awareness of my own interests or of what it is to be self-interested. Also, one may wonder if the capacity to act prudently is necessary to act justly, whether, once we know what the interests of others are, and, given we do not have the capacity to act prudently, we could act justly towards these people. I think from such issues we should steer clear; but at least with our analysis, it becomes clear what types of problems may be generated.

Let us now turn to Lewis' non-genetic or conceptual account of the transition from rational prudence to rational justice. A key passage is the following:

> The first imperative of reason may be regarded as prudential only and directed to the consequences of action for ourselves. But already the implication of respect for others is contained within it. Criticism of action by reference to self-interest alone still bespeaks a rightness or a wrongness which is objective in the sense that if this action is to be regarded as rationally justified in one's own case, then it must have the same justification for every other rational being under like circumstances. Thus it is a basic condition of human association that each recognize as right that only in his conduct toward his fellows which he is satisfied to recognize as similarly sanctioned in their conduct toward himself.[52]

If this can be accepted, we get a much more plastic view of the relationship between justice and prudence. While prudence and justice are two distinct critiques and technically justice overrules prudence in conflict, we are made more aware of their conceptual affinity here. There is no indication in D4 or D4' that S is aware that his acting as he does at t is a rational activity. If we can at least assume that he recognizes that there are other rational beings in the world, it will be important for us to characterize his acting prudently in a way that, with the additional assumption, he will recognize the legitimacy of the prudential aims of others. We thus modify D4 accordingly and get:

D_5 *S acts prudently at t*=df   At *t, S* acts to promote a life good on the whole for himself, having felt constrained to consider, and having considered, the consequences of his act for his life in determining how to act, and in these considerations finding no alternative way of acting that might more likely promote a life good on the whole by increasing total satisfactions; *S* is aware that his activity is rational.

Prudence is now defined, but more needs to be said about its ground, taking into account what emerged from our investigation into why be prudent — that observations concerning human nature play a role in establishing the ground of *any* imperative. We thus devote ourselves in Chapter 3 to a more general discussion of imperatives and their ground.

FOOTNOTE REFERENCES FOR CHAPTER 2

[1]C.I. Lewis, "An Attempted Answer," *Values and Imperatives,* edited by John Lange (Stanford: Stanford University Press, 1969), p. 72

[2]C.I. Lewis, "The Meaning of Liberty," *Values,* p. 148.

[3]C.I. Lewis, "Practical and Moral Imperatives," *Values,* p. 148.

[4]Ibid., *p. 139.*

[5]*C.I. Lewis, "Subjective and Objective Right," The Collected Papers of Clarence Irving Lewis,* edited by John D. Goheen and John L. Mothershead, Jr. (Stanford: Stanford University Press, 1970), p. 192.

[6]*Ibid.,* p. 192.

[7]*Ibid.,* p. 192.

[8]*Ibid.,* p. 193.

[9]C.I. Lewis, "The Individual and the Social Order," *Collected Papers,* pp. 204-205.

[10]*Ibid.,* p. 205.

[11]*Ibid.,* p. 205.

[12]C.I. Lewis, *GNR* (New York: Columbia University Press, 1955), p. 56.

[13]C.I. Lewis, *AKV* (La Salle: The Open Court Publishing Co., 1946), p. 397.

[14]C.I. Lewis, "Values and Facts," *Values*, p. 101.

[15]C.I. Lewis, "An Attempted Answer," *Values*, p. 72.

[16]John Rawls, *A Theory of Justice* (Cambridge: The Belknap Press of Harvard University Press, 1971), p. 408.

[17]*Ibid.*, p. 409-410.

[18]*Ibid.*, p. 413.

[19]*Ibid.*, pp. 420-421.

[20]*Ibid.*, p. 416.

[21]*Ibid.*, p. 417.

[22]*Ibid.*, p. 421.

[23]*Ibid.*, p. 421.

[24]Lewis, *AKV*, p. 481.

[25]Charles S. Peirce, "Definition and Function of a University," *C.S. Peirce: Selected Writings*, edited by Phillip P. Wiener (New York: Dover Publications, Inc., 1958), p. 332.

[26]Lewis, *GNR*, p. 40.

[27]*Ibid.*, pp. 11-12.

[28]Lewis, *GNR*, pp. 84-85.

[29]*Ibid.*, p. 85.

[30]*Ibid.*, pp. 85-86.

[31]John S. Mill, *Utilitarianism* (New York: The Liberal Arts Press, 1957), p. 39.

[32]Lewis, *AKV*, p. 553.

[33]C.I. Lewis, *MWO* (New York: Dover Publications, Inc., 1929), p. 91.

[34]*Ibid.*, p. 90.

[35]*Ibid.*, p. 112.

[36]*Ibid.*, p. 103.

[37]*Ibid.*, p. 102.

[38]*Ibid.*, "Appendix C," *passim*.

[39]*Ibid.*, p. 408.

[40]*Ibid.*, pp. 408-409.

[41]Immanuel Kant, *Critique of Pure Reason*, translated by Norman Kemp Smith (New York: St. Martin's Press, 1929), pp. B391=A394 and B93-B94=A68-A69.

[42]Lewis, *GNR*, pp. 11-12.

[43]*Ibid.*, pp. 81-83.

[44]*Ibid.*, pp. 83-84.

[45]*Ibid.*, p. 83.

[46]*Ibid.*, p. 82.

[47]*Ibid.*, p. 82.

[48]*Ibid.*, p. 40.

[49]C.I. Lewis, *OSI* (Bloomington: University of Indiana Press, 1957), pp. 91-92.

[50]Lewis, *GNR*, pp.83-84.

[51]*Ibid.*, pp. 10-11.

[52]Lewis. "The Meaning of Liberty," p. 148.

CHAPTER 3
HUMAN NATURE AND THE GROUND OF IMPERATIVES

We here explore human nature with an eye to its relevance for establishing the ground of any rational imperative, prudential or otherwise. Once committed to dealing with imperatives generally, the question arises as to what type of activity is subject to evaluation by imperatives. After isolating the predicates that Lewis thinks describe such activity and discussing their relations, a sketch of the various critiques or sets of imperatives, is provided. We then begin our characterization of human nature and divide that effort into two main parts. In the first we concentrate on the relationships between knowing and doing and bring out an essential feature of humans. We further explore human nature in a discussion of rules and objective facts. Finally, we show how our dealings with human nature can be brought to bear on the problems of establishing the ground of the right.

I

Lewis connects what is right and what is imperative; right connotes critique[1] and critique is in accord with *a* critique or system of imperatives that spells out what is right or wrong for a given mode of activity. Thus when Lewis begins to puzzle over what it signifies to speak of the imperative[2] and to seek out its root senses,[3] he is simultaneously interested in the root senses of the right in general, as rightness is rooted in some corresponding imperative to conduct ourselves in a certain manner.[4] This approach, Lewis says, contrasts with the Kantian enterprise that primarily focuses on moral rectitude. Lewis feels that if we begin with a single mode of the right, like justice, we may lose out on an understanding of the right in general and fail to see that the moral imperative or some other, like the prudential, is part of a more general imperative.[5]

The first thing to establish in dealing with imperatives generally is what sort of activity we can depict as right or wrong, *i.e.*, what activity is subject to evaluation by imperatives. It might be noted that Lewis sees such activity as being identical with that activity for which one can be held responsible. Thus we alternatively may see the project as one of detailing the notion of activity for which one can be held responsible. We will first indicate the various predicates as candidates for this description and then work out their interrelationships and entailments. Now, Lewis uses different combinations of predicates to describe activity that is subject to evaluation by imperatives. Sometimes it is characterized as activity that is decidable and determinable by deliberation.[6] In other passages, Lewis adds that it is activity that is corrigible and subject to critical assessment.[7] There are other places where he leaves out that it is behavior capable of being deliberated but adds that the doer can be called upon to justify it in addition to its being done by decision and being subject to criticism.[8] Finally, we find that there is a characterization of activity that is subject to imperatives of right as "whatever is corrigible, decidable, subject to deliberation, self-governable."[9]

Self-governable activity might be understood simply as activity capable of according with imperatives; decidable, activity which we can make a reasoned decision to undertake; corrigible, capable of being corrected; and deliberable, capable of being reasoned about. We assign no particular predicate to that which the doer can be called upon to justify.

Let us now look at these predicates or terms that are used to characterize self-governable activity with an eye to working out their relationships. The main point that emerges is that we are obliged to accept them in some package and that no one of them is enough to characterize the activity in question. We begin with "decidable". We already said that if one can reach a reasoned decision concerning some activity, then it is decidable. From just this we see that some deliberation could be involved, thus decidable activity is deliberable. If some error is pointed to in how we arrived at our decision, we suppose that the next time we have a similar decision to make, the error can be corrected, that the decidable activity is corrigible. But it is not clear that all decidable activity is activity that we can call upon the doer to justify; I have children in mind when I make this claim. Some activity may indeed be decidable, yet we do not feel we can require a justification of it. It may seem correct to describe as decidable, deliberable, and corrigible the activity of a three year old who has stuffed himself with cookies minutes before his dinner, although the appeal of the displeased parents of "Now why did you do that?" is hardly to be taken literally.

We turn now to the phrase, activity that the doer can be called upon to justify. I would like to characterize a situation where it makes sense to ask, concerning the activity involved, "Why did you do that?" but where the activity was not decidable, deliberable, or corrigible. Suppose a prestigious physician is addressing a large group. The doors to the room are open and it is evident to anyone walking by that an address is being given. During the talk a passerby unknown to others in the room walks past the doors, looks in as he passes, and as he passes, makes a loud, quacking sound. After the talk, a member of the audience sees the passerby and takes the occasion to ask why he did that, calling upon the passerby to justify his perverse activity. The reply by the passerby is to the effect that he has a vocal disorder in which he cannot control these ouybursts. We can well imagine that the member of the audience might reply that he is sorry to hear of this impairment without apologizing for his original question or giving any indication that he thought it was out of order.

As with activity that one can be called upon to justify, activity characterized simply as deliberable activity need not be corrigible, decidable, or such that one can be called upon to justify it. Any activity that is thought about counterfactually is deliberable, yet some of this activity displays none of the other attributes. What sense does it make to say that my pipedreaming, for example, is corrigible and decidable activity?

We come finally to corrigible. While we may agree that any corrigible activity is decisionable and deliberable, I think corrigible activity falls short of entailing all the attributes involved for a reason similar to that offered for decidable. Again, while the activity of a child may be corrigible, it is not clear that we will call upon him to justify it. I think it becomes clear from this sketch of the interrelations of the predicates under discussion that no one alone is enough to characterize activity for which we are responsible. Some package deal is involved. Minimal descriptions of such activity are (1) decisionable along with that which we can call upon the doer to justify and (2) corrigible along with that which we can call upon the doer to justify.

Lewis' discussion of liberty makes precise inroads into this consideration of how we are to characterize activity for which one can be held responsible and our future dealings with human nature: "Liberty. . .consists in the exercise by the individual of his *natural capacity* for *deliberate decision* and self-determined action."[10] On Lewis' view, if one did not exercise his capacity for self-determined action (which is what liberty is), he would have no personality.[11] Exercising that capacity, says Lewis, is the only way for one to maintain his individuality.[12] In this way we might understand liberty as the *ratio essendi* of personality. On the other hand, that one is an individual and is aware of himself means that he knows that he can act in accord with deliberate decision and that he is free:

> Man is born free in the sense that he discovers
> himself as an individual in discovering that this
> ability to act by deliberate decision belongs to

his nature.[13]

And this is why we might understand personality as the *ratio cognoscendi* of liberty. It might be noted that at times Lewis equates freedom with liberty (and in the preceding quotation he has). He does, however, on some occasions, contrast man's liberty quite sharply with an animal's freedom; he speaks of animals as having a physical freedom to act according to their impulses as opposed to the way we have characterized a man's liberty or human freedom above.[14]

To this point little has been said to bring out the more dynamic aspects of liberty where man's liberty increases, says Lewis, as his exercising that capacity increases. Lewis asserts that the capacity in question increases when more concrete possibilities become open to the individual for realizing his ends and he seizes these possibilities.[15] The claim is that as man's understanding of his enviroment increases along with his knowledge of objective facts, of the options, and resources made possible by his social order, in tandem with the assumption that he adjusts his activity accordingly through deliberate decision, he becomes freer; his liberty increases. What we end up with is a picture of man and his environment where man's freedom develops as he, in part, works toward an understanding of his environment; man's capacity for liberty is itself a natural capacity; it is part of his nature as a human. But he cannot exercise this capacity without acting on a deliberated decision which involves his apprehension of his situation in his enviroment. Lewis' account of freedom, then, portrays a fundamental aspect of human nature and is closely tied to his position on activity that is subject to evaluation by imperatives.

II

Haing resolved to examine the entire scope of self-governable conduct, the question of just what it encompasses arises. Lewis holds that this activity allows for a two-fold division — determinations of correct concluding and believing and determinations of correct doing[16] — both of which have corresponding critiques of correctness: logic and ethics. According to Lewis determinations of correct concluding and believing are prior to determinations of doing, and the latter presupposes the former.[17]

While the moral or ethical critique may be thought of as the major critique in determinations of correct doing, there are others. (It should be noted at this point that Lewis uses the term "moral critique" to refer to two things: (1) the ethical critique and (2) all of the critiques of doing.) They include the prudential and the technical. The technical might be thought of

40

as consisting of any rules or imperatives that govern our conduct for which we are responsible that are not already part of the critique of prudence or ethics.

Just as we saw that the ethical is not the sole critique that deals with determinations to do, so too is it the case that determinations of believing and concluding do not fall solely under the governance of logic or the critique of consistency. Parts of the cognitive critique, which we suppose handles determinations of empirical fact, include cogency as well as consistency.[18] Cogency is the broader mode and consistency is presupposed by it. Basically our critique of consistency tells us whether whatever is under consideration is logically possible; and cogency, whether it is likely or true:

> There are, in fact, two distinguishable modes of cognitive critique — one narrower and one broader, the latter presupposing or including the former. The narrower, directed to determining whether what is entertained can be or could be representationally correct and have assignable objective reference, is the critique of consistency, the formulation of which is deductive logic. The broader critique, directed to determination of the veracity of objective reference, or the nearest approximation to that which is attainable — a warranted degree of probability — represents what epistemology should aim to formulate.[19]

In *GNR*, because cogency is the broader mode of the cognitive critique, Lewis speaks of the critique of consistency as being "part of the critique of cogent thought."[20] Furthermore, it might be noted that we said earlier that determinations to do presuppose determinations of fact. Now we can add that it is the case that determinations to do also presuppose cogency: "Any critique of action presumes a critique of cogency as antecedent."[21] Thus, in our two main modes of determination of fact and action (doing) — cogency is presupposed.

If any critique of action presupposses a critique of cogency, and hence of our beliefs, some relationship is evident. Let us now make it explicit. Perhaps the most revealing statement concerning this relationship is that "when we criticize an act, what we criticize is the doer's commitment because it is this commitment which is the doing of it."[22] In this way any

41

rightness of self-governed doing is hardly separable from the question of rightness of some believing which is implicated in this doing.[23] It should be made clear that Lewis is using the term commitment in a peculiar way. He is not referring to some state of mind in which the doer has decided and perhaps feels obligated to act in a certain way but rather to the first stage of the actual doing of the act where the oomph of initiative is so great that there is no turning back; the act has begun; and we go on to call this the doing of the act.

Lewis subscribes to this view for the following reason. When the doer is considering how to act, the cheif peculiarities of acts that allow him to select among alternative acts are their consequences. Consequences that are intended, hoped for, feared, those that are actual, probable, and possible provide the only ground for specifying an act.[24] In saying that when we criticize an act, we criticize the doer's commitment, all that is being said is that we base our criticism and evaluation on the same considerations that the doer used in selecting the act — consequences. Since commitment to act is the first stage of doing the act, it is arbitrary whether one speaks of criticizing the doing or the commitment, as long as it is clear that the basis of the criticism is consequences.

What Lewis is employing here is the Peircean *thought-belief-action* model, where thought is for the purpose of belief, and action is the final upshot of belief. Peirce tells us that it is the irritation of doubt that initiates our thinking. Doubt arises when some area of our experience becomes unsettled, when we have a problem. Thought on the matter begins and continues in order to provide a solution and relieve us of the annoyance created by the doubt. And thought on the matter stops when we have, or think we have, solved the problem, when we have some belief on the matter. Peirce is somewhat unclear, however, on what is involved in the transition from belief to action. "Belief does not make us act at once, but it puts us into such a condition that we shall behave in a certain way, when the occasion arises."[25] We might look at Lewis' view as specifying more clearly what is happening at that part of the Peircean continuum where action occurs. Lewis introduces the dimension of the commitment of the act, given that he is primarily concerned with characterizing activity for which one can be held responsible, and is thus interested in what there is about activity that we can *evaluate*.

With this background on the right , critique, and imperatives, we can go on to our discussion of human nature in search of a ground of imperatives. We gain insight into Lewis' understanding of human nature through his descriptions of human, active, or rational beings. (Let us refer to such beings as humans unless we are paying particular attention to one of these predicates.) The claim of paramount importance among Lewis' observations is that humans cannot be described accurately without mention of their capacity to foresee consequences of action as well as to guide their activity in this knowledge. The claim is that man's knowledge of objective fact is intimately connected with directives of doing, or, alternately, that principled action is an essential human trait. This draws on Lewis' view that there is never any fundamental distinction between knowing and doing. Apprehension of certain objective facts results from our having interacted with, and having attempted to order, our environment. And our reason for wanting to know is for the sake of informed, future action. Lewis, like Dewey, rejects the model of the passive being's being affected by his environment and then packaging and processing the data to obtain knowledge.[26]

Now each of Lewis' characterizations of humans draws on his view that man can and should act with reference to what he knows. The "nature of man as an active being" involves the fact that "he is capable of self-government," and he "determines whatever he does deliberately by reference to what he thinks, and what he expects as consequences of what he chooses to do."[27] "A rational being is one who is capable of deliberate decision and recognizes it as imperative to conduct himself by the advise of cognition, giving it precedence over his affective impulsions and inclinations."[28] The prevailing motif is that humans cannot be described adequately without mention of their capacity to foresee consequences of action as well as to guide their activity with this knowledge. Man's apprehension of objective fact is interwoven with directives of doing in such a way that what he knows about his environment signals what he must do.

Let us explore this aspect of human nature in more detail and look closely at how Lewis further characterizes the relationship between the factual and the imperative. In "Pragmatism and the Roots of the Moral" we find that "empirical statements *give rise to* imperatives."[29] "Imperatives *are implicit* in particular empirical facts" is Lewis formulation in "Practical and Moral Imperatives;"[30] and "the command. . .*originates* in the fact itself," in "Turning Points of Ethical Theory."[31] One further statement that is revealing and to the point is that "our sense of the imperative *is* simply our sense of fact."[32] An example of Lewis' is of some help in perceiving the single idea he is trying to convey with such statements. Lewis asks us to consider the statement of objective fact, "The stove is hot." According to Lewis,

> that the stove is hot means, amongst other things, that if you touch the stove, you will be burned. Hence the indicative statement which advises of the fact likewise advises, 'If you do not want to be burned, don't touch the stove.[33]

Lewis develops this example further in "Pragmatism and the Roots of the Moral;" he refers to it here as a "little paradigm:"

> 'The stove is hot.' That is the announcement of objective fact. . . .
>
> 'If you touch the stove, you are likely to be burned.' That spells out one implication of a consequence of action contained in 'The stove is hot — one possible verification of the objective fact as announced.
>
> 'If you do not want to be burned, don't touch the stove.' That is the advice of action contained in 'The stove is hot' and correlative with 'If you touch the stove, you are likely to be burned.' It merely translates this last into the grammatical form of advice, using the imperative mood in the apodosis.[34]

Paradigm this is. In the course of a few sentences Lewis adumbrates his views not merely on the kinship of facts and imperatives but also on facts and their verification. Let us consider each of these phenomena in more detail. Lewis' stance on the meaning of objective claims in *An Analysis of Knowledge and Valuation* provides the ground for developing the full-blown account of his view of the verification of objective fact. The view is that any objective statement of fact strictly implies an infinite number of terminating judgments or tests that set out means of verifying the claim. The set of tests so implied is the meaning of the objective claim. Each test has the form, under conditions C, if one performs action A, event E obtains. Thus, with respect to the objective claim,

(1)   The stove is hot.

terminating judgments like the following are stictly implied:

(2a) If you touch the stove, you are likely to be burned.

(2b) If you place a pan of water on the burner, it is likely to boil.

(2c) If you lay a candle on the stove, it is likely to melt.

Besides tests like (2a) - (2c) being contained in (1) are hypothetical imperatives like:

(3) If you do not want to be burned, don't touch the stove.

In effect, Lewis is asserting that the same coin of objective fact signals its verification on its one side and its advice for human action on the other, the entire coin being forged from the same experience. That we do glean from the statement of objective fact advice valuable for the direction of conduct is a function of our nature as humans.

IV

I am now prepared to investigate the relevance, if any, this discussion of human nature has for establishing the ground of any first imperative of right. Lewis' treatment of this matter comes out most clearly in his refutation of one skeptical of there being such valid imperatives. Lewis' project of forcing the skeptic into an untenable position consists of two complimentary strategies, both drawing on his view of human nature. On the one hand, Lewis offers what he refers to as a Kantian deduction. Whereas Kant found it necessary to posit the categories of the mind to account for our phenomenal experience, Lewis brings out that the possibility of human experience hinges on valid rules of practice. Without them, the human might be seen as a creature that merely responds to immediate feelings and affections, an animal that is not faced with decisions requiring deliberation, intelligence and rationality, which involve the apprehension of objective facts and the conforming of action to their advice respectively:

I suggest that explicit apprehension of objective facts. . .is the essence of what we call intelligence. Human experience is human by being for us an apprehension of more than is to be observed immediately. . .I should now like to suggest that the government of behavior according to what we know to be objective fact, and not according to the way we feel, is the root

45

character of what we call rationality....To be
rational is to govern behavior according to what
we know and not simply according to how we
feel — that is, to *govern* behavior and not merely
allow ourselves to be moved by impulse, inclination, and emotion.[35]

Besides this "deduction," Lewis offers *ad hominem* appeals against the
skeptic, and sometimes, as we shall see, characterizes them as a *reductio ad
absurdum* against the skeptic. Basically, I think what Lewis refers to as his
argumentum ad hominem has what I shall refer to as a constructive and a
destructive moment, both of which deviate from the sophistical nature of the
traditional *ad hominem* argument. What I call the destructive moment most
closely parallels the traditional *ad hominem* argument, and, more specifically,
the circumstantial *ad hominem*, which might have the following as the
paradigm case.[36] A Christian minister holds that Christ did not rise from the
dead. It is pointed out to him that he should not hold this *because* of the
circumstances he is in — because he is a Christian minister, he should stand
by the scriptures that clearly state that Christ rose from the dead; the truth of
the claim is not considered.

Now, Lewis wants to argue against a skeptic who repudiates valid.
imperatives of right doing.[37] Basically, the skeptic is told that if he expects
anyone to accept his claim, then he will have to recognize valid principles of
right and wrong. In a sense, the argument can be seen as proceeding much
like the *ad hominem* concerning the minister. The skeptic should not assert
that he expects others to believe his conclusion, for, *being* a skeptic, given the
circumstances he is in where he is arguing against valid norms, he should
not argue for the validity of the conclusion he wants others to believe. But
here the similarites with our paradigm end. In our paradigm something
illicit seems to be going on; to be sure Christian teachings are inconsistent
with Christ's not rising from the dead, but the reason the minister is asked to
abaṅdom his view is simply because of his circumstances and not his other
beliefs; he is not told or shown that he holds that Christ rose from the dead
and Christ did not rise from the dead. In the case of the skeptic, however,
when it is pointed out to him that because he *is* a skeptic, he should not hold
that he can convince others, what is being said is that because of his *beliefs* as
a skeptic, he cannot consistently hold that he can *convince* another of
anything. But when the argument takes this turn, some inconsistency has
been pointed to. The skeptic seems tacitly to subscribe to the very thing he is

denying and we have what appears to be a *reductio*. Thus we find that the destructive moment of Lewis' *ad hominem* seems to escape the sophistical nature of the traditional *ad hominem* and serve as some legitimate piece of arguing against the skeptic. So much for the destructive moment.

Although Lewis never explicitly mentions the similarities between this destructive *ad hominem* and a *reductio*, he does draw the parallel between what I call the constructive *ad hominem* and a *reductio* in "An Attempted Answer." Here a *reductio* is referred to as an *ad hominem* argument *because* an implicit premise about the *nature of man* is included:

> But I should wish it to be observed that in that kind of *reductio ad absurdum* which I think holds against any theory which is skeptical of the validity of normative judgments, I appeal to certain premises as implicit. This type of argument is, as I have acknowledged, also an *argumentum ad hominem* — *ad hominem* in the sense in which 'Hominem' may be spelled with a capital and means to denote the genus homo. It appeals to facts about the common nature of man which are open to all of us in a reflective examination of the kind of creatures we are, and which I think that any such examination which is judicious must compel us to recognize as the truth about ourselves. The *reductio ad absurdum* which proceeds by exposing an implicit pragmatic contradiction must, in the end, appeal to such self-consciousness of active and self governing creatures.[38]

It is this aspect of Lewis' *ad hominem* argument that I have been referring to as the constructive moment and I think operates as an independent argument against the skeptic. Lewis is now using observations about the nature of man for his *reductio*. Because of the significant role they play in the *reductio*, he plays on words and calls it an *ad Hominem* argument with a capital "h," drawing attention to "homo" and the important observations about human nature rather than indicating the use of any classical *ad hominem* argument. It is here that our earlier discussion of human nature becomes operative, for without the observation that an essential feature of man is that he directs his activity in accord with imperatives, the *reductio* would not be possible. We recall that the peculiar feature of man is his capacity for self-directed activity. And this in part depends on his ability to grasp objectively the actualities of his world and to recognize and pay heed to the imperative advice that issues forth from the facts he apprehends. If the *reductio* is dependent upon a certain supposition about human nature and that in effect involves our assuming that there are various imperatives of right doing and thinking, and in addition that is what we are ultimately trying to show, can it not be said that Lewis is begging the question? Yes, and Lewis admits this:

> But if, in view of the acknowledgments I have
> just made, you should be minded to say that my
> whole argument now stands revealed as not
> only an *argumentum ad Hominem* (spelled with a
> capital 'H') but also a *petitio principii*, I shall not
> attempt to fend off that accusation. . . .[39]

Just what the status of Lewis' *reductio* is in his ethics is not clear. We find, on the one hand, its being seemingly freed from association with *petitio principii* and its being recognized as a legitimate proof for the validity of principles of right doing, while on the other, its association with *petitio principii* and ultimately its inefficacy is stressed. Let me make this clearer. Concerning the independence of the *reductio* from *petitio*, Lewis claims that "the only conclusive proof of the validity of the basic principles of right is a kind of *reductio ad absurdum*. . .,"[40] that "I would recognize that the basic imperatives cannot be argued for without *petitio principii*, but only that manner of *reductio ad absurdum* of their denial. . . ."[41] Similarly, "any argument in support of rightness and imperatives of any kind must be *petitio principii*, except only for the fact that whoever *refuses* acknowledgment of these validities must then discover himself in a pragmatic contradiction,"[42] which is the thrust of the *reductio*. Again, all of these statements seem to free the *reductio* from an association with *petitio*.

In seeming contrast to these passages, we find text that taints even *reductio* with *petitio*, that "such proof by the method of *reductio ad absurdum*, when addressed to ultimates, must be, in a queer kind of way, a begging of the question."[43] More specifically, as to the ultimates of logic, Lewis claims that "any argument to the conclusion that there is such a thing as validity in argument is obviously a kind of *petitio principii*,"[44] that "any attempt to demonstrate first principles of logic would inevitably be *petitio principii*."[45] But these specific observations are not peculiar to logic, we find, when we flesh out the above quotation:

> In consequence, what is most general, most comprehensive in its scope, most nearly ultimate, concerning any topic, cannot be proved at all, unless by some manner of observation or some *reductio ad absurdum* of denying it. And though it may not have been generally remarked, it is nevertheless the fact that even such proof by method of *reductio ad absurdum*, when addressed to ultimates, must be in a queer kind of way, a begging of the question.[46]

Here it seems that *reductios* end up as *petitio principii*. We are thus in need of some means of harmonizing Lewis' statements concerning his *reductio* (or his *argumentum ad Hominem* or what I have referred to as the constructive moment of his *ad hominem* argument).

I think one cogent way of construing what Lewis has said that saves the appearances and allows for a consistent reading is this. Lewis sees his *reductio* for the existence of some norms as different from a formal, direct argument. Now, for Lewis, *petitio principii* is a fault with formal, direct arguments. We thus find Lewis, on the one hand, *contrasting* his *reductio* with arguments (direct) that are *petitio principii* and suggesting that his *reductio* is free from any sin of begging the question; *strictly speaking*, it would be a category mistake to say that his *reductio* begs the question. On the other hand, we find Lewis going on to *associate petitio principii* with his *reductio* but qualifying that the question is begged "in a queer kind of way."[47]

I believe all of this may become even clearer if we look more closely at the pragmatic contradiction that Lewis thinks is involved with the *reductio*. We can actually isolate two such contradictions, both of which deviate from contradictions in any strict sense where contradictory propositions are asserted. On the one hand we find that it is in the very assertion of the skeptic's claim, which we assume is meant to have significance, that the inconsistency arises.[48] It arises from what he is saying and doing. He says there are no norms, yet what he is doing when he says this is trying to *convince* us that he is *right*, which indicates that he subscribes to some norms of thought. Of course, no argument in any strict sense could allow actions and not simply propositions to be admitted as premises; thus we begin to see Lewis' reasons for contrasting formal arguments with the *reductio* he is considering. The other pragmatic contradiction again involves the skeptic's denial of there being any valid norms but this time ultimately draws on what we can reasonably expect anyone, including the skeptic, to subscribe to concerning an analysis of human nature, namely, its rule-guided character. This, as Lewis says, is implicit in the *reductio* and thus there is never any formal but only pragmatic contradiction.

If it is now clear why formal, direct arguments might be contrasted with the *reductios* in question, we can consider how these *reductios* may, in *some* sense, beg the question. What we attribute to the skeptic, either because of his motives for asserting his skepticism of the validity of normative rules or because of what we expect anyone to agree to concerning human nature, is the very thing we are interested in showing in our argument against the skeptic. Thus we have a begging of the question. But again, it is only of a sort, since what we attribute to him never formally appears as a premise.

Throughout this discussion of Lewis' constructive and destructive *ad hominem* arguments, we have mentioned several times that we are interested in refuting a skeptic (and ultimately to establish a ground of right) although we have not been careful to distinguish between one skeptical of any rule or one skeptical of just some, like the moral or prudential. The two types of skeptics can be discussed in this order. As to the first, what I propose is to construct an argument against a universal skeptic, drawing on what Lewis calls his observations about human nature. The resulting argument, I think, takes us further than leading one skeptical of there being any valid rules into pragmatic contradiction. In a sense, then, we will be improving on Lewis' constructive *ad Hominem*.

I find two passages that seem to be attempts to answer the question Lewis raises, "But why *rules*?"[49] In both passages Lewis seems to answer by making *observations* about human nature, and it seems that this is the status he wants them to occupy. (We recall from the quotation above that statements about what is most general about a certain topic, if provable, depend upon either an observation or a *reductio*; and clearly *reductios* are not involved here.) In fact, after answerinf the question "Why rules?", he writes, "in observing this fact. . ."[50] One of Lewis' answers to the question revolves around man's inability to govern his behavior in any other way:

> Men can direct their action to foreseeable ends
> only by reference to some explicit or implicit
> generality — because they can do nothing in
> this world except by applying to the present or
> future something learned in the past, and this is
> possible with respect to a newly presented or

anticipated situation only so far as it is subsumable in some class with past like cases. We know how to bring about what we can expect to happen in the present case only because it is what has happened in past like instances. In consequence , a directive which failed to have such generality — failed to be of the form 'In cases such-and-such, do so-and-so' — would be quite impossible for any human mind to frame or utilize. We act according to some implicitly formulatable rule or we do not direct our action to foreseeable ends at all.[51]

In "The Rational Imperatives" we find that:

Men can direct their action to foresecable ends only by reference to some explicit or implicit generality — because they can do nothing in this world except by applying to the present or future something learned from the past, and this is possible with respect to a newly presented or anticipated situation only so far as it is subsumable in some class with past like cases. We know how to bring about what we can expect to happen in the present case only because it is what has happened in past like instances. In consequence, a directive which failed to have such generality — failed to be of the form 'In cases such-and-such, do so-and-so' — would be quite impossible for any human mind to frame or utilize. We act according to some implicitly formulatable rule or we do not direct our action to foreseeable ends at all.[51]

In "The Rational Imperatives" we find that:

No doing of so-and-so on occasion such-and-such is intelligible as anything other than some generality, both with respect to the so-and-so and with respect to the such-and-such.[52]

Now, it seems that some of what Lewis is saying here about humans may first be stated more abstractly as characteristics of the nature of rule-guided activity or of what we mean by certain key concepts involved with such activity, making no reference yet to any specific actors, let alone to humans:

(1) If one applies the past to present or foreseeable future ends to direct his action, he must classify aspects of the present or future with the past to direct his action.

(2) If one directs his action by classifying aspects of the present or future with the past, he is acting in accord with implicit or explicit directives of doing (rules).

At this point we might enter *some* of Lewis' portrayal of human nature from the quotation above:

(3) Humans direct their action by applying the past to present or foreseeable future ends.

Following from (1) and (3), *modus ponens*, we get:

(5) Hence, humans act in accord with implicit or explicit directives of doing (rules).

What we end up with is an argument that allows us to show that human activity is essentially rule-guided without starting off with a characterization of human activity as being such. Of course some argue that all deductively valid arguments beg the question or never allow us to learn something new from them; all is implicit in the premises. But it seems that we need not worry here about such a move being made by the skeptic we are dealing with. For, if he tried to argue for the validity of this or any point, we could lead him into pragmatic self-contradiction as Lewis did above; he who tries to convince us of any point presupposes valid rules of arguing and thus cannot maintain as a general theory that there are no valid rules. We thus see the cogency and brilliance of Lewis' more general means of handling the skeptic. Nevertheless, it does seem that the argument offered above can be seen as another means of dealing with the skeptic in a fashion that does not crush what we have seen to be the spirit of Lewis' attempt to ward off skeptical attacks by drawing attention to our nature as humans.

We turn now to one skeptical of some particular imperative like the moral or prudential. For one thing, Lewis accuses such a person of being inconsistent. Acting in accord with imperatives is part of acting as a rational human being. Because the foundation for imperative activity is involved with the sciences and logic is the same as for ethics, one who is skeptical only in ethics, for example, should, to be consistent, maintain a skeptical attitude toward logic and science,[53] which he does not. Further, because he is falling short of recognizing what it is to be rational, he is irrational:

> In the case of the moral, I can only say finally that one who does not acknowledge it as imperative to behave in that same way in which he would call upon other men generally to behave is irrational, as one who denies the law of contradiction is irrational, and one who should find prudence a matter of no concern is irrational.[54]

Furthermore, with regard to the moral skeptic, in particular, Lewis offers that "he can only be persuaded with a club,"[55] and that he should be banished from our company.[56]

Let us now look more carefully at the sort of inconsistency attributed above to the moral skeptic. It seems that an argument of this sort is operative. All rational imperatives are similar in that they all have the same ground, the same relation to our active attitude as humans. Accordingly, if there is something wrong with one of them that leads us to "negate" it, all of them must similarly fall. The model involved in such an argument is one of some whole entity's losing its integrity if any one of its parts does. Without argument, it is unclear why we should embrace such a model when dealing with imperatives. Formally, because one negates one imperative, he is not commited to negating all. A whole — parts model where the lack of a part is construed simply as that thus seems more palatable. Drawing on this, we can still criticize one skeptical of some rules, saying that he displays a lack or privation. It should be noted that this manner of dealing with the skeptic of some particular imperative or critique does not preclude our leading him into some pragmatic self-contradiction and thereby point to some inconsistency.

In fact, such arguments against skeptics of the critiques of ethics and of consistency are suggested by Lewis. Briefly, the skeptic of the moral is commited to a view that other people do not constitute a relevant factor that he must take into account in his self-governed activity. Yet this view itself takes others into account in some way. As for the skeptic of logic, how could he expect to convince anyone of his position were he not himself subscribing to principles of correct inference? The point is that skeptics of sundry sorts can be led into pragmatic contradiction. Now if one skeptical of some particular imperative cannot be led into such a contradiction, we saw that there is still the move open of attributing a lack to him. And that, we recall, depended on our earlier analysis of what it is to be human, for without an understanding of what a human is, we cannot speak of human privations.

We thus find that an understanding of man's nature is central to various arguments Lewis launches against skeptics of some or all rules. That human nature is the ground of the right means that it is natural for man to act in a rule-guided fashion, the rules being the reference points by which right and wrong, in any of their many modes, are determined. This is not to say that this characterization of man's nature embraces every relevant dimension. It was a sufficient characterization for our purposes of dealing with those skeptical of various directives. But we have said very little, if anything, of man and the quality of his association with others in a society, of the integral relationship between the individual and his society, and of the role of the moral law in these considerations, each being elements of the chemistry of human nature. It is with this that we will concern ourselves in the next chapter.

FOOTNOTE REFERENCES FOR CHAPTER 3

[1]C. I. Lewis, "Turning Points of Ethical Theory," *The Collected Papers of Clarence Irving Lewis*, edited by John D. Goheen and John L. Mothershead, Jr. (Stanford: Stanford University Press, 1970), p. 215.

[2]C. I. Lewis, *GNR* (New York: Columbia University Press, 1955), p.71.

[3]*Ibid.*, p. 59.

[4]C.I. Lewis, "Subjective and Objective Right," *The Collected Papers*, pp. 201-202.

[5]Lewis, "Turning Points," p. 216.

[6]*Ibid.*, p. 215.

[7]Lewis, *GNR*, p. 78.

[8]Lewis, "Turning Points," p. 217.

[9]C.I. Lewis, "Pragmatism and the Roots of the Moral," *Values and Imperatives*, edited by John Lange (Stanford: Stanford University Press, 1969), p. 108.

[10]C.I. Lewis, "The Meaning of Liberty," *Values*, p. 146.

[11]*Ibid.*, p.146.

[12]*Ibid.*, p. 146.

[13]*Ibid.*, p. 146.

[14]*Ibid.*, p. 147.

[15]C. I. Lewis, *OSI* (Bloomington: University of Indiana Press, 1957), p. 54 and p. 67.

[16]Lewis, *GNR*, p. 18.

[17]*Ibid.*, p.19.

[18]C.I. Lewis, "The Rational Imperatives," *Values*, p. 165.

[19]*Ibid.*, p. 165.

[20]Lewis, *GNR*, p. 47.

[21]Lewis, "The Rational Imperatives," p. 166.

[22]Lewis, *GNR*, p. 47.

[23]*Ibid.*, p. 43.

[24]*Ibid.*, p. 47.

[25]Charles S. Peirce, "The Fixation of Belief," *C. S. Peirce: Selected Writings*, edited by Philip P. Wiener (New York: Dover Publications, Inc., 1958), p. 99.

[26]John Dewey, "The Reflex Arc Concept in Psychology," *Philosophy, Psychology, and Social Practice*, edited by Joseph Ratner (New York: Capricorn Books, 1965), pp. 252-267. Dewey here breaks down old models of human behavior where behavior is explained in terms of a subject's first passively receiving stimuli, which may be presented to him accidentally by his environment or are purposively given to him by some other agent, and then responding in some way. Dewey replaces this with a model where, at best, stimuli and responses are teleological constructs that allow us to temporally identify segments of an act. His new model is one of a coordinated sensory-motor circuit where seeing is, *e.g., for the sake of reaching.* On Dewey's model, the desired "response" gets built into the "stimulus."

[27]C.I. Lewis, "An Attempted Answer," *Values*, p. 63.

[28]Lewis, "The Rational Imperatives," p. 167.

[29]Lewis, "Pragmatism," p. 119, my italics.

[30]C.I. Lewis, "Practical and Moral Imperatives," *Values*, p. 138., my italics.

[31]Lewis, "Turning Points," p. 223, my italics.

[32]*Ibid.*, p. 221.

[33]*Ibid.*, p. 223.

[34]Lewis, "Pragmatism," p. 118.

[35]*Ibid.*, pp. 116-118.

[36]Irving Copi, *Introduction to Logic* (New York: The Macmillan Co., 1961), pp. 55-56.

[37]Lewis, "An Attempted Answer," p. 66.

[38]*Ibid.*, pp. 79-80.

[39]*Ibid.*, p. 81.

[40]*Ibid.*, p. 64.

[41]Lewis, "The Rational Imperatives," p. 168.

[42]Lewis, "Practical and Moral Imperatives," p. 132.

[43]Lewis, "An Attempted Answer," p. 81.

[44]Lewis, "Practical and Moral Imperatives," p. 130.

[45]Lewis, "The Categorical Imperative," *Values*, p. 196.

[46]Lewis, "An Attempted Answer," p. 81.

[47]*Ibid.*, p. 81, my italics.

[48]Lewis, "Practical and Moral Imperatives," p. 131.

[49]Lewis, "Pragmatism and the Roots of the Moral," pp. 119-120.

[50]*Ibid.*, p. 120, my italics.

[51]*Ibid.*, p. 120.

[52]Lewis, "The Rational Imperatives," p. 162. I think Lewis' point is quite clear. I do, however, have one major objection to his remarks. I assume that when Lewis is speaking of bringing the past to bear on a newly presented situation, he is speaking of some essential feature that cases of the past share with this present case and is not making the trivial claim that *something* of our past experience is always brought to bear on new situations that we are confronted with. It seems that such a view does not allow for innovative behavior or creative solutions to problems that do not draw essentially from the past for a solution. Clearly we can direct our activity to a given end and not essentially base our plan of action (rules for behavior) on past experience. Consider, *e.g.*, plans for non-violent defense on a *large* scale. There are no precedents in the past that could guide us to such a goal, yet plans have been created to reach the state of affairs where our defense is essentially non-violent in nature. Although what I have said here may seem compatible with this quotation from "The Rational Imperatives," it is the case that the preceding quotation, to which my criticism is more appropriately directed, is a later, and apparently more precise formulation of Lewis' view.

[53]Lewis, "Practical and Moral Imperatives," p. 128.

[54]Lewis, "An Attempted Answer," p. 82.

[55]Lewis, *GNR*, p. 59.

[56]*Ibid.*, p. 59.

CHAPTER 4
SOCIETY AND THE DEMANDS OF JUSTICE

I

Lewis' moral imperative, one formulation of which we discussed in chapter one, is Kantian, and we can perhaps best appreciate Lewis' by considering what he found to be the strength of Kant's and how he circumvented the weaknessess associated with Kant's. Kant, of course, advised that we "act only according to that maxim by which you can at the same time will that it should become universal law."[1] Lewis recognized as a virtue of this moral rule that it is "formulated ways of acting, maxims, subordinate but still general rules, which are the subject matter which the categorical imperarive may operate upon as critique."[2]

As to the difficulties with, or the various attacks that critics have levied against, Kant's moral rule, it has been pointed out, for one thing, that sometimes no specific duties can be derived from the imperative. Also, too little guidence is offered for formulating the maxim. Third, moralists of varying persuasions, like egoism and altruism, seem to be able to justify their activity with Kant's imperative as could a fanatic justify despicable modes of activity. Lewis does make specific reference to some of these difficulties and makes the appropriate emendations for his Kantian imperative. Some of the objections above turn out not to be problematic for Lewis, while others can be worked out with the conceptual apparatus he has provided for us.

The first two problems mentioned are interrelated. Suppose I am deciding whether to break a promise. I might recognize that if I broke my promise, it would lead to the demise of the institution were everyone to act according to the maxim, "Break promises." But suppose I formulate a more specific maxim and take into account the dynamics of my situation. I owe a wealthy friend five dollars today. I have only five dollars today and will not be paid until tomorrow. Now it is the case that I have a family; some of the children are ill. Paying the friend back means no dinner for the family. A more specific maxim may be "Break a promise when it involves postponing payment of a small sum to a rich man and sick children may become sicker if the promise is not broken." The universalization of this maxim does not seem to endanger the institution of promising. Yet why should I deal with this maxim rather than the first or any other that may be descriptive of my situation? And if I have no criterion by which to choose the proper maxim, how can I ever have a specific duty assigned by the categorical imperative?

Lewis' Principle of Equality Before the Moral Law seems to handle the problems of specific duties and conflicting maxims:

> Take no decision of action which is a member of
> any class of decisions of doing all members of
> which you would call upon others to avoid.[3]

First of all it is clear that, from a formulation of this sort, one would not expect Specific duties to be provided at all, whereas the Kantian formulation invites this sort of criticism; Kant's directive is to act in a certain way. Lewis' imperative leaves open what particular course of action is taken, as long as it is not forbidden. Another advantage of this formulation is that it does not involve us in the formulation of a maxim for the situation at hand; we are working with classes of decisions. It should be noted that this move of Lewis' is not simply a facile answer to ward off an objection to Kant. It fits in with Lewis' general convictions about rules that they are to leave some room for choice and should not completely determine the situation to which they apply.

Now one may object that rational activity proceeds in accord with rules, and although we are given some guidance from Lewis' revision of the Kantian imperative, our location of a particular decision to act in some class is done without the guidance of rules and is thus arbitrary and irrational. This, however, is wrong-headed. We may not be aware of the principles of organization that we employ when we sort a stack of colored cards into piles of blues, reds, and greens. But we do not need to infer that one could not be formulated or that we were not acting in accord with a rule or rules. On like reasoning, while we may not be cognizant of the explicit rule that allows us to assign a particular decision to a particular class, that does not mean that one could not be formulated or that we were not acting in accord with a rule.

The situation is very similar to what has been described as legal reasoning, where we are concerned with whether the instant case shares relevant similarities with cases decided in the past. Of course in the courts one case may be very similar to past cases, yet it is decided differently because of a new perception of how to deal with some problem. For example, in the early history of products liability, the party injured by a defective product was required to be in privity of contract with the manufacturer in order to have standing to sue for damages; a remote purchaser, say one who purchased from the original purchaser of a product, could not hold the manufacturer liable for injuries caused by the defective product. Then one court, aware of changing social attitudes, perceived that the manufacturer should be answerable for injuries sustained by anyone who might reasonably be expected to use the product. This marked a break from treating like cases in this field of products liability in a similar manner. Subsequent cases sharing similarities with the newly decided case become part of a new likeness class; it has as its unifying feature what originally led the court to decide a case differently from the longstanding precedent.[4]

If legal reasoning so described can be seen as a rational process, so too can moral reasoning when we deal with classes of decisions of doing. We expect new classes to form as we factor out different features of these decisions as relevant. As an example, most members of a particular culture at a particular time may find stealing in any form abhorrent and would place any decision to steal in a class of all decisions to steal, all members of which they would call upon others to avoid. We might then imagine there is some citizen who is deciding whether to steal and sees a relevant difference between his decision to steal and other decisions to steal which he would call upon others to avoid. It may involve stealing when one is in great need from one who is very wealthy as opposed to stealing from a poor man. This, of course, does not justify his decision — he is to consider whether his decision will fall in *any* class, all members of which he would ask others to avoid. If it does not, his placing instances of the poor deciding to steal from the rich outside the class of decisions to steal, all members of which he would call upon others to avoid,creates a new class. Other similar decisions to steal may fall into the new category, and, in the future, he may see his decisions to steal from the rich (as long as he remains poor) as being a member of a class of decisions that he would not mind others to make, thus reinforcing the alteration of the class of prohibitive decisions to steal. It is in this manner that moral reasoning proceeds when one is guided by Lewis' categorical imperative. As such, it seems no less a rational process than that involved in the construction of any likeness classes.

As for the criticism that "any philosophical egoist [could] crawl under the Kantian tent," Lewis is not disturbed; the egoist can crawl under his too:

> As a fact a convinced and consistent egoist
> could be a completely moral man, respecting
> others as he asks that they respect him. It would
> be required of him only that he acknowledge

exactly the same manner of egoistic conduct as
right also for everybody else.[5]
Similarly, the altruist could conform to Lewis' imperative. The crucial thing
to observe is that the moral law does not dictate the precise degree to which
we take others into account; it does, however, require that we do so to some
degree. We expect the egoist will have limited associations with others;
there are few things that he expects from them and wants no more from
others in their treatment of him. On the other hand, we picture the altruist as
being sensitive to a large class of the needs of others and responds to them in
addition to his expecting that others will do the same for him.

Lewis does try to indicate the implausibility, however, of these representatives of diverging moral persuasions taking refuge under his tent. In
arguing against the egoist, Lewis offers a weak and a strong attack. As for the
former, in "Practical and Moral Imperatives," he phrases his claim, without
argument, in "it-seems-to-me" language: "I do not myself see how an egoist
can genuinely respect the experience of others as the reality which it is and
still hold to his position."[6] On the other hand, in GNR we find that the egoist
is "contraindicated by his misapprehension concerning the possibility of a
good life under such conditions."[7] Lewis offers Hobbes' insights of the self-
defeating characteristics of egoism to support this, Lewis' moral law being
unable to do the job.

Furthermore, in GNR, he identifies the problem with universal altruism.
Universal altruism, he argues, does not allow for maximum individual
happiness for two reasons: (1) It does not allow for competition. (2) It does
not allow for one's deciding "private matters on private grounds."[8] As for
the first, Lewis points out that we cherish some competition and competition
is possible only if our own good is put before the good of others at times,[9]
which is not allowed for by universal altruism.

If we back off somewhat from Lewis' critique of egoism and altruism and
observe just what sort of appeals he is making to bring out their difficulties, it
becomes clear that he is essentially making reference to the goodness of the
consequences involved with egoism or altruism. Egoism and altruism are
disparaged because they do not provide us with the good consequences we
want. This seems to suggest that, although the egoist and the altruist may
formally meet the requirements of the moral law, we can still resort to other
grounds to show the weakness of their positions.

In what follows I will make clear that good and bad consequences are
taken into account by Lewis' moral law and that this allows us to deal with

the egoist, the altruist, and the fanatic under the same rubric. We already saw that one might think it a weakness of the Kantian imperative that it allowed us to call egoists and altruists just men; yet we also observed that this did not bother Lewis. Furthermore, we intimated earlier that the most heinous of acts could be justified under the guidelines of Kant's categorical imperative. One may then wonder whether Lewis, in allowing an egoist and an altruist to seek justification under his imperative, has also let the fanatic slip in. I think in one sense he has, but not unwittingly. There is nothing in Lewis' Principle of Equality Before the Moral Law that would preclude a firm believer in the aims of the Third Reich from justifying his activities. But all this means is that the fanatic has met the condition of consistency of action. But this is not the only requirement of the moral law according to Lewis.

Besides the "formal and explicit" criteria that the fanatic can meet, there are "contextual and implicit" criteria in the moral law. They involve "what is implicit in reference to 'you' " and turn on two factors: (1) "that acts are to be judged according to their good or bad consequences"[10] and (2) "that such good or evil of their effects is to be assessed from the viewpoint of those upon whom these effects are visited."[11] Since the formal and explicit criteria are not the only criteria in Lewis' moral law, one can be indifferent as to what sort of activity satisfies these, as long as he can rule out undesirable activity with the implicit criteria.

Let us look more closely at how good consequences are to be dealt with in relation to the moral law. There is no automatic procedure whereby, given the imperative and various decisions to act, one can determine whether the act is right or wrong, according to the rule. "No rule, by itself, can forthwith determine any act as right or wrong to do except as the specification of the act considered includes circumstances by reason of which the rule is pertinent."[12] What it is about the circumstances of an act that we are interested in is whether or not good consequences follow from the act. In addition, the rule involved will not be without reference to the good or evil that the act may produce. Lewis speaks of this good or evil as being similar to that which the major and minor premises of a syllogism have in common — "some term in common."[13] The apparatus we have, then, in deciding upon the rightness of some decision to act is:

> Moral Law (includes implicit reference to goodness in consequences)
> Decision to act with statement of goodness of its consequences

Correctness of act

On Lewis' view, the decision to act that is in question is to meet the formal requirements of the moral law; in addition, on a cogent prediction of its social value, it should produce more good than ill consequences. With this model, Lewis is able to outline how one might overcome some of the major objections to Kantianism and Utilitarianism. A fanatic whose activity is essentially harmful to others cannot assert that his activity is permissible when the full moral syllogism is employed, whereas he may be able to meet the formal requirements of Kant's or Lewis' imperative. On the other hand, simply a calculation that some act produces a greater balance of good over evil than any of its alternatives is never sufficient to determine whether it is to be permitted. Thus, although the greatest good may result from punishing an innocent man, under some unusual circumstances, we can still question the legitimacy of the act on Lewis' view unlike on the traditional utilitarian position which has us consider only the greatest good for the greatest number. We thus find that Lewis, in overcoming some of the obstacles to Kantianism, incorporates features of utilitarianism into his view and at the same time is able to handle problems traditionally associated with utilitarianism.

Earlier in our analysis we distinguished between two senses of "moral." Any self-governed activity was construed as moral activity (call it moral$_1$) as was activity that met the formal requirements of the moral imperative (moral$_2$). We should now make two more senses clear — "moral" referring to activity that responds to the entire moral syllogism (moral$_3$) and "moral" referring to activity that also meets the higher ideals of love of our neighbor and benevolence that are not commanded by the moral imperative (moral$_4$).

Let us look more closely at this final sense. Lewis speaks of its relation to the moral imperative in the following passage:

> Thus what the law of justice requires is mutual respect, not love: it does not command that the individual be equally concerned for others as for himself, but only that he respect the freedom of others in acting. . . .Consonantly, although this law of mutual respect is a basic moral principle, it is to be doubted that it provides. . .a sufficient ground for the whole of morals. Nevertheless it does constitute a sufficient critique for those

62

public and social institutions which affect the liberties of men — because, admitting the higher command that men love one another and the moral obligation to conserve the ends of other's equally with one's own, still that higher law is not one the observance of which any man can demand of another toward himself, or would wish to see socially enforced, if social enforcement of it were conceivable.[14]

Lewis is here dealing with an enriched notion of moral behavior having as its requirements a love of our fellow man and an equal interest in his goals, neither of which his moral critique fully encompasses.

The most Lewis feels his ethics does to accommodate this aspect of morality is to make the critique of morals at least compatible with these loftier duties:

But as far as I desire, or feel it my duty, to treat other persons not only as behaving objects present in my environment but also as ends in themselves, I have an interest, which cannot be abstracted from, in the absolute quality of their immediate experience. The importance of such interest is commensurate with the significance of love and duty in human life.[15]

It might at this point be objected that Lewis, in trying to establish rational foundations for ethics and show its commonality with other cognitive disciplines in order to avoid the positivists' claim, has gone to the opposite extreme and has bifurcated rational justice and emotions that enter into moral activity. But while it is true that, alone, the law of justice does not dictate love, it is possible, as we saw, that it may allow for a moral command to love others to operate in conjunction with the moral law.

Also, I think it can be argued that Lewis' claim concerning why one would not expect the moral law to dictate benevolence, especially considering its application to any positive system of laws, is very similar to Bentham's observation that the enforcement of beneficience is better left to the sphere of private ethics or prudence rather than to legislation. According to Bentham, the public enforcement of the positive virtue of beneficience, that has as its motives sympathy and benevolence, would at times involve the legislator in punishing where punishment is not due or in having to make

63

decisions as to punishment in areas where an accurate judgment is difficult or impossible. The ill consequences of enforcing beneficience outweighed the good, on Bentham's view. Lewis' basic revision of Bentham in this regard, then, is to have observed that his moral law formally does not demand benevolence while Bentham used his moral principle, the Principle of Utility, to decide how to deal with benevolence in his moral system.[16] One further thing should be brought out concerning Lewis' treatment of benevolence and the moral law. With Kant, benevolent conduct toward others was not considered moral conduct. Acting out of benevolent motives was not compatible with acting morally. In making the two compatible, Lewis paves the way for a society of enriched social relationships that he feels are important but cannot be commanded.

To this point we have been considering the moral imperative from the viewpoint of its being a command that directs the activity of individuals and what is involved in that direction. Another dimension through which we will want to consider it is in terms of its conceptual affinity to Lewis' views of society and social value. We have already broken ground in this area in this final consideration of the moral law and its implication for our association with others.

II

A central theme appearing in much of Lewis' writings is the importance, if not the indispensability, of individual initiative and decision to society, on the one hand, and of socializing features provided by society for the individual, on the other. The fundamentals of both aspects of this motif can be stated concisely. Concerning the significance of the society for the individual, Lewis mentions, among other things, that we would not consider one a civilized individual if it were not for his being brought up in society.[17] He needs the skills and information that others can transmit to him. Lewis' point is dramatized by accounts of those who have developed outside of society. As we mentioned earlier, there are accounts of wolf-children,[18] children who were individually isolated from any contact with a society in their early years and upon their return to the civilized world were found to be virtually incapable of acquiring a language, of internalizing the social mores, and of developing their rational faculties. Says Lewis, "There is the fact that moral and other rational insights, like other forms of learning, call for, and benefit from, social reinforcement."[19]

Lewis points to other ways society can aid the individual, although no claim is here made that such assistance is essential to individual develop-

64

ment. For one thing, when an individual aligns his aims with those of a large, well-working institution, the probability of his achieving his goal is greater.[20] If one is interested in philosophizing, for example, he may find it difficult to devote much time to that enterprise if the society did not approve of an individual's philosophizing nor have as one of its values supporting a class of philosophers. His main occupation probably would not be philosophy; he would need to support himself by means other than philosophizing. He may find difficulties in obtaining books that he thinks important to read. He may be cut off from current philosophical discussions in other societies, and so on, the point being that it is unlikely that he would ever achieve a goal of doing serious philosophy. Another benefit of society to the individual that Lewis points to is that individual thinking, when done in a social context, is accelerated and often corrected.[21]

Lewis' main argument concerning the necessity of individuals for society is that without individuals, the society would freeze. Lewis is not saying something trivial here — that one needs people for a society. He is contrasting individual persons with individuals who are persons that are free to think and act and are not part of a society where they must perform as social insects. The claim is that innovations and progress in a society depend on free individuals.[22]

Now it may be objected that this line of reasoning fails to show the indispensability of the individual to society, assuming that Lewis has in mind that *all* in the society are to be individuals. Consider a society where most of the people are, through no choice of their own, laborers, contributing virtually nothing to the intellectual resources or progress of the society. They have little or no chance for social mobility and a fairly clear-cut picture of their unchanging role in society. Also imagine this society to be endowed with sizable intellectual resources, of freely acting and thinking individuals who ingeniously direct the masses, devising innovations for the good of all. Clearly nothing about such a society is contradictory or inconsistent, yet it would be difficult to imagine its coming to a standstill. Indeed we characterized it as progressing. What I am getting at is that Lewis' argument above may seem at most to argue for some free individuals and that a society filled with such people is not needed to prevent its freezing.

In "The Individual and the Social Order" we find, however, that Lewis is making a claim about a just or moral society, that he is employing a normative concept of society. A more explicit statement of Lewis' position is that if a civilization is to be just, it must have as its members free individuals, for only autonomous, self-governing men are capable of acting morally and a society is a civilization whose members can act justly towards one another:

It is by individual freedom of thought and the respect for the individual in his own initiative and self-criticism, that human society has become human instead of an ant colony. Only the self-governing and self-criticizing animal is human and could be moral.[23]

I think that we can formulate three propositions based on several passages from Lewis' works that serve to make his normative concept of society clearer:

(1)   If there is no freedom and self-direction, then there is no society.[24]

(2)   If there is no society, then there is no moral sense.[25]

(3)   If there is no moral sense, there is still the possibility of society's continuing.[26]

It might be noted that the phrase, moral sense, does not refer to a faculty but simply to some common sentiments, one being that justice is required.

Now if there is a door open for the survival of a society that stands in danger of destruction, I assume it revolves around some feature that is essential for society. We find such a feature in (1). But how could mere individual freedom and self-direction rescue the society with no moral sense? While freedom underlies the moral sense,[27] freedom does not vanish with the moral sense. That freedom and self-directed activity are the saviors of society in the event of the loss of the moral sense entails man's acting morally and maintaining his individual moral autonomy. Thus, even in a society with no moral sense, men are to act morally if there is to be society.

Lewis' point now becomes clearer. He wants to build into the notion of a society some degree of just action of one man to another. There is no society if there is no justice involved. And with such a conception of society, the counter-example offered earlier now seems misdirected, as we would not consider a grouping of people, where many are not free to direct their own activity, a society. Of course Lewis never *says* that *all* in the *society* are to be free individuals, but we suppose that given that he is employing a normative concept of society here, the members are at least capable of behaving in a way commensurate with what we isolated as an essential feature of a society; they are free to conform to the moral imperative. In this consists the

66

conceptual affinity, which we mentioned earlier, between Lewis' moral imperative and his notion of society.

We can learn one final thing about Lewis' view of a society by considering his characterization of social value. For Lewis, social value cannot be a category or concept that selects as its members or instances those things that are valuable to all in a society. For on such a view, the root thesis of Western civilization is undermined and the way is paved for a totalitarian government that draws on such a view of social value. Western civilization is predicated on the idea that whatever is of value to some, and does not produce ill effects for others, has some degree of social value. This in turn rests on respect for the individual and for his chances of achieving a good life.[28]

The structure of Lewis' argument for this position is relatively simple. Either social or impersonal value involves value for some (and perhaps all) or only for all. The second disjunct is false. Hence, the first. His denial of the second draws on an insight he attributes to Herbert Spencer — that no matter how useful it may be to speak of a society as some single organism or entity, it is only a manner of speaking. "Humanity. . .has no central consciousness."[29] One arguing that the first disjunct is false is probably drawing on this misleading metaphor. How could something be of social value if it is not of value to the entire society? Surely one does not say that a scarf is of value to one's neck. But if one does not conceive of society as some sort of organism, he need not think that society as a whole or all of its parts need to be gratified or experiencing value before one can establish that something is of social value.[30]

Some have criticized views such as Lewis' which aim at making room for an essential feature of Western civilization — that what is of social value need not be of value to all. They have argued that such a view goes hand in hand with a doctrine of ethical relativism. In a democracy, there can be no doctrine of absolute values if the majority's determining what is best is to be justified. Whether an action is right or wrong depends on whether it produces value. Since values are relative to the determination of the majority, right and wrong too are relative. Others, disturbed by the claim that a democracy rests on a doctrine of ethical relativism, have argued that although there may be no absolute values in a Platonic sense, there are indeed some "authentic values" that those in a democracy must subscribe to; the legitimacy of government is offered as an example.[31]

Lewis subscribes to no doctrine of absolute values yet is committed to no ethical relativism. While members of the society may disagree over what is of value, and we want to allow that these valuings are of social value, Lewis embraces, as we have seen, a normative view of society, where its members are capable of acting in accord with a moral imperative that sets the conditions for right action towards others in the society; the moral imperative, while it takes good and bad into account, has an independent function in determining right and wrong which is not simply a function of what is good or of value. Here, we again see how Lewis' value theory and his theory of right are working together for a unified view. In the last chapter we will want to look at what the essential components are of an ethics that has such features and where such an ethics stands in relation to other positions taken in the history of Western ethics.

FOOTNOTE REFERENCES FOR CHAPTER 4

[1]Immanuel Kant, *Foundations of the Metaphysics of Morals,* translated by Lewis White Beck (New York: The Bobbs-Merrill Co., Inc., 1959), p. 39 = p. 422, Akademie edition.

[2]C. I. Lewis, "The Categorical Imperative," *Values and Imperatives,* edited by John Lange (Stanford: Stanford University Press, 1969), p. 200.

[3]C. I. Lewis, *GNR* (New York: Columbia University Press, 1955), p. 93. This Principle of Equality Before the Moral Law is a part of the moral imperative that we formulated at the end of Chapter 1. That imperative, which we said was the socially significant counterpart of the Law of Objectivity, is divided into two. On the one hand, we have the Law of Compassion which governs our relations with other sentient beings: "Recognize in your action affecting any sentient being that claim on your compassion which comports with its capacity to enjoy and suffer." On the other, we have the Law of Moral Equality. Lewis never formulates this but indicates that it involves respecting others as ends and allowing each to determine his actions as long as no harm to others results. The Principle of Equality Before the Moral Law, according to Lewis, is the "morally more important implication" of the Law of Moral Equality.

[4]See Edward H. Levi, *Introduction to Legal Reasoning* (Chicago: University of Chicago Press, 1948).

[5]C. I. Lewis, "Practical and Moral Imperatives," *Values,* pp. 142-143.

[6]*Ibid.,* pp. 142-143.

[7]Lewis, *GNR,* p. 95.

[8]*Ibid.,* p. 95.

[9]*Ibid.,* p. 96.

[10]C. I. Lewis, *OSI* (Bloomington: Indiana University Press, 1957), p. 93.

[11]C. I. Lewis, "Pragmatism and the Roots of the Moral," *Values*, pp. 114-115.

[12]Lewis, *GNR*, pp. 83-84.

[13]*Ibid.*, pp. 10-11.

[14]C. I. Lewis, "The Meaning of Liberty," *Values*, pp. 149-150.

[15]C. I. Lewis, *MWO* (New York: Dover Publications, Inc., 1929), pp. 407-408.

[16]Jeremy Bentham, "Of the Limits of the Penal Branch of Jurisprudence," *Introduction to the Principles of Morals and Legislation* (New York: Hafner Publishing Co., 1948), *passim*.

[17]C. I. Lewis, "The Individual and the Social Order," *The Collected Papers of Clarence Irving Lewis*, edited by John D. Goheen and John L. Mothershead, Jr. (Stanford: Stanford University Press, 1970), p. 214.

[18]Jean-Marc-Gaspard Itard, *The Wild Boy of Aveyron, Wolf Children and the Problem of Human Nature*, edited by Lucien Malson (New York: Monthly Review Press, 1972), *passim*.

[19]Lewis, *OSI*, pp. 94-95.

[20]Lewis, "The Individual and the Social Order," pp. 210-211.

[21]Lewis, *OSI*, pp. 95-96.

[22]*Ibid.*, pp. 106-107.

[23]Lewis, "The Individual and the Social Order," p. 214.

[24]Lewis, *OSI*, p. 77.

[25]Lewis, "The Individual and the Social Order," p. 207.

[26]C. I. Lewis, "Ethics and the Present Scene," *Values*, p. 4.

[27]Lewis, "The Individual and the Social Order," p. 208.

[28]Lewis, *GNR*, p. 71.

[29]C. I. Lewis, "Turning Points of Ethical Theory," *The Collected Papers*, pp. 220-221.

[30]This is also discussed in "The Individual and the Social Order," p. 210.

[31]Charner Perry, "Ethics and Democracy," *Ethics*, (vol 83, no. 2, 1973), pp. 89-91.

CHAPTER 5
CONCLUDING REMARKS —
THE COMPONENTS OF A NATURALISTIC THEORY OF JUSTICE

In some passages, Lewis tells us that he wants his position in ethics to be taken as an ethical naturalism, and he raises the question of its compatibility with ethical rationalism to which he also claims to subscribe.[1] According to Lewis, ethical naturalism involves the claim that "no act can be determined as right or wrong without reference to the consequences of it as good or bad."[2] Now a characteristic of ethical rationalism that Lewis thinks may be antithetical to ethical naturalism is the "thesis that right and wrong are indeterminate except by reference to rules and principles, principles themselves including reference to the good or bad as essential to determining what specifically they dictate."[3] But ethical rationalism, as characterized here, seems to be a view completely encompassing Lewis' characterization of ethical naturalism. It is unclear just why there is any question of their compatibility.

In "Practical and Moral Imperatives," however, Lewis casts his ethical naturalism differently, and it has the *prima facie* appearance of conflicting with ethical rationalism. He asks whether "this account [of valuation (my insertion)] — which I have ventured to characterize as 'naturalistic' and 'pragmatic' — will prove compatible with recognizing any valid ground of obligation to others or any moral imperative."[4] Here the question is not posed in terms of the compatibility of one theory of obligation with another, where one simply seems to encompass the other, but rather in terms of whether a naturalistic theory of values is compatible with a rationalistic theory of obligation, the combination resulting in a naturalistic ethics. It is the question asked in this way that we will explore in an attempt ultimately to place Lewis' move in ethical theory in perspective and indicate why it might be characterized as a naturalistic theory of justice.

Included in Lewis' naturalism in values are two major claims. One is that we have experiences that are unmistakably satisfying, a claim of *de gustibus non est disputandum*. The ordinary man is, in his experience, confronted with satisfactions, and his experience of such value stands in no need of correction.[5] Also included in this view is a meta-ethical claim concerning the status of value judgments — that the means by which we assess value or through which we arrive at our value judgments are of the same kind that we employ in making any cognitive claim; objective claims of what is good and bad enjoy the status of objective claims in the sciences; there is no fact —

value dichotomy. The theory of obligation that Lewis subscribes to might be characterized briefly in this way. Ethical right and wrong is formally a property of one's decision to act conforming with an imperative having as its ground human rationality itself. The imperative makes an essential reference to the good and bad consequences of the act in question and requires that they be taken into account before any final determination of right or wrong is made.

Now when the two positions are presented in this way, there seems to be no question of their compatibility. I think that what Lewis probably had in mind when he construed their compatibility as a problem was that one generally conceives of a rationalistic theory of obligation in a far more extreme form than Lewis. And given this, they might initially think it implausible to combine it with a naturalism in values. Let me make this clearer. One's initial intuitions about a rationalistic theory of obligation probably involve ethical right or wrong's being determined solely by an act's conforming with an imperative. On this line of reasoning, any determination of human good would be unnecessary in determining one's obligations. But as we pointed out, Lewis' view is not this extreme. Given that Lewis sees Kant's ethics as almost exclusively comprising a theory of justice,[6] in tandem with the observation that Lewis has incorporated with the Kantian view his value theory and aspects of utilitarianism (reference to objectively good consequences as part of the determination of right and wrong) to naturalize a Kantian theory of justice, we might refer to Lewis' position as a naturalistic theory of justice.

In an effort to place Lewis' theory in perspective, I provide for the reader a chart that details the main moves that can be made in developing theories that relate the right and the good and that relate desires and values. Historical fillers are suggested for some of the combinations. It is of no particular consequence whether the reader agrees that there is some sense in which the various combinations should in fact be filled by the various representatives that I have suggested, the main aim being to illustrate where Lewis' move lies relative to the main moves that are available.

71

	Whatever is desired is good.	Some things desired are good.	The relation between desires and good is indeterminate.
Right is determined essentially by reference to good.	HOBBES	MILL	MOORE
Right is determined in part by reference to good.		LEWIS	
Right is exclusive of good.		KANT	

The top line of combinations has as representatives prominent British philosophers. We might understand by Hobbesian egoism the position that whatever is desired is good; the objects of one's self-interests alone are desired; hence the objects of one's self-interests alone are good. One's obligation is to maximize this good and his action is right if this obligation is fulfilled. Now, Mill, a utilitarian, is committed to a hedonistic value theory, suggesting that pleasure or happiness alone is desired, and in this consists the good. However, he also wishes to maintain, and devotes some considerable time to reconciling with this position, the view that virtue is a good, is worthy of being desired, while recognizing that some do not desire it. He wishes to hold that, even in this case, virtue is, and should be seen as a good, and thus it seems that, under such circumstances, we can say that, for Mill, only some things desired are good. For Moore, good is a nonnatural property and thus is not explicable in terms of one's desires. The right is simply that which is a means to the good.

The continent's representative is Kant, who agrees that human goods are those things that are desired but also holds that the only thing that is good in itself is a good will which is not among the human goods. Thus, only some things that are desired are good on his view. The morally correct action involves one's acting from a sense of duty towards the maxim that conforms to the categorical imperative.

We can now turn to the position Lewis occupies on the chart. On Lewis' value theory, those things we say are good have a foundation in what we desire. But some satisfying experiences cannot be referred to as objectively good if we do not know how to bring them about in the future. Thus, only some things desired are good. And as we have seen, the moral imperative directs us to consider the goodness of the consequences of any decision to act, and, in accord with the chart, for Lewis, right is determined in part by reference to good.

Lewis warns that "in philosophy, brevity invites dogmatism,"[7] so it is with some hesitation that I conclude that, in short, Lewis takes a position in ethics mid-way between a Mill and a Kant.

FOOTNOTE REFERENCES FOR CHAPTER 5

[1] C. I. Lewis, *GNR* (New York: Columbia University Press, 1955), p. 97.

[2] *Ibid.*, p. 97.

[3] *Ibid.*, p. 97.

[4] C. I. Lewis, "Practical and Moral Imperatives," *Values and Imperatives*, edited by John Lange (Stanford: Stanford University Press, 1969), p. 126.

[5] C. I. Lewis, *AKV* (La Salle: The Open Court Publishing Co., 1946), p. 398.

[6] C. I. Lewis, "Subjective and Objective Right," *The Collected Papers of Clarence Irving Lewis*, edited by John D. Goheen and John L. Mothershead, Jr. (Stanford: Stanford University Press, 1970), p. 190.

[7] C. I. Lewis, "The Rational Imperatives," *Values*, p. 156.

SELECTED READINGS

"The Rational Imperatives"

In philosophy, brevity invites dogmatism. The purpose of this essay will be to suggest considerations which, if more adequately developed, might figure as prolegomena to ethics. But if, for brevity, these are set down in summary form, I hope it will be understood that they are not dogmatically meant.

Man is the self-conscious animal, capable of self-criticism and of doing by deliberate decision. His activities, as compared with those of other animals, are more largely governed by his knowing, by apprehension of objective fact and considered prediction rather than by apprehensive feeling merely and other affective conditioning of his responses. Man has learned to respond in this more complex and consciously directed manner; he has also learned that this mode of response has superior reliability in securing conformity of the results to his desires. Supposedly, when a tiger sees a man, it tends to do just what seeing the man makes it feel like doing. But when a man sees a tiger, he has learned not to be too precipitate in doing what that makes him feel like doing. Obviously that is not the whole story nor wholly true, but on balance it seems to be the gist of the matter. This capacity to look before leaping and to take a second thought must be a critical consideration in accounting for the fact that men have succeeded in killing most of the tigers instead of the tigers killing most of the men. This ascendancy over the other beasts of prey by a creature which, biologically, is not too well equipped for close combat is the most compelling evidence that rating our human mentality as higher is not a mere product of human self-conceit.

The task of ethics is, or should be, to elicit and formulate the acknowledged or acceptable principles of man's criticism of himself in action. In the nature of the case, criticism is pertinent only to such acts as are or may be done by self-direction and deliberately, since it is these only which may be altered by critique. The attentive second glance, or more prolonged consideration before commitment, is the deliberation of the act.

However, the critique of acts is not confined to those which in point of fact are deliberated. Often what we do is within our power to decide in the sense that it could have been restrained if question of its desirability had occurred to us, though no such doubt did in fact call attention to it. Such acts are corrigible, whether deliberated or not. Most frequently, corrigible acts are done from habit; actual deliberation of them is the exception rather than the rule. But the very fact that we are creatures of habit, and aware of that, leads us often to criticize such actions *ex post facto*, and to take to heart the results of such criticism. We may so decide to do differently on any future like occasion, or not to be so thoughtless next time. For reasons of this sort, all corrigible acts are customarily classed together and spoken of as deliberate. We shall here adopt this less strict but more frequent and more important usage of 'deliberate act.'

It is of some importance to examine the character of deliberated actions, since these set the model for our critique of all deliberate acts. Every deliberated act has a mental part and a physical part. (The word 'act' will here be restricted to activities which eventuate in some physical doing: mental activities will be mentioned later.) There is first the envisagement of something as possible for us to bring about — sometimes of more than one such possibility. In any case, there is the alternative of doing or not doing. There is then attentive consideration, briefly or at length, terminating in decision. Criticism of action mostly turns upon characters of the decision or of what is so decided. But the decision is not the doing, since we may decide to do something tomorrow or next week and meantime change our minds. The "doing itself" is the indescribable "oomph" of initiation, the fiat of the will, accompanied by expectation of something as about to follow. This fiat of willing is the commitment because prior to that any deliberate act can be altered or canceled, but after that the act and all its consequences are out of our hands. What so happens physically has, as a first part, some movement of the doer's body. This is always regarded as part of the "act done," but seldom as the whole of it. Which further consequences of the fiat of willing (further events which follow but would not have come about without it) are regarded as part of the act, and which are spoken of instead as "consequences of the act," is a matter with respect to which our usage varies from case to case. The bodily movement in throwing a stone, for example, will be expected to have different consequences according as water or a window or a human head is observed to be in the expected line of flight; and stone throwing is regarded as a different act under these different circumstances. Characteristically we tend to name the act by mention of those consequences of the fiat of willing which are desirable or undesirable and hence important on their own account, or those which are important for the criticism of it. Also we sometimes name the act by its expected consequences even if they are not actual, *e.g.*, "Tom threw a stone at John," or by reference to actual consequences, even though they were not expected, *e.g.*, "Tom cut himself with his knife."

The consequences of physical doing are not, of course, confined to the physical. The most important results of action are likely to be its eventual consequences for the doer's experience or that of others.

Some deliberate acts are elementary and some complex. An act is elementary if there is no physical first part of it which can be done without doing the whole of it. A complex act is some series of elementary acts each of which is such as could be done separately. But a single fiat of willing may be determinative for a complex act: after initiation it may run itself off, chainwise, without further attention. Also an act so complex as to require some series of separate initiatives may still be determined upon by one decision.

We know how to do a complex act by knowing how to do each constituent elementary act. But we know how to do an elementary act only in the sense of being able to produce the bodily movement at will. The connection between this fiat of the will and the occurrence of the bodily movement is inscrutable. That a physiologist may be able to describe it as some series of physical happenings is beside the point; he does not thereby become able to initiate a first part of it without the rest — or if he does, then it becomes for him a complex act. In any case, the connection between the fiat of the will and the physical happening remains as inscrutable to him as to the rest of us.

By virtue of this inscrutability of the connection between the fiat of willing and what is sequent upon it, no contemplation of an act in advance of doing can have any content other than expected consequences of willing, and none which is criticized after the doing can be so criticized except by reference either to its expected or to its actual consequences. Apart from consequences, there is no manner in which an act done or to be done can be specified, and no character of it to be critically considered.

Turning to the mental part of the act: the intention of it is the entertainment, in advance, of those consequences expected to follow from the fiat of willing, and the intention includes all consequences which are expected, whether these are actually sequent or not. The purpose of the act is that part of the intention (in exceptional cases it may be the whole) for the sake of which it is adopted. Only those consequences which the doer desires to bring about are attributable to him as purposes, but any anticipated result, whether desired or not, will be said to be something intentionally done. The word 'motive', as applied to acts, is ambiguous, even as used by students of ethics; and we shall here avoid that word. But particularly in thinking of

Kant, for whose ethical theory motives are centrally important, it may be desirable to consider what is so intended. Plainly this does not coincide with what is spoken of above as the purpose of the act — expected and desired consequences. I suggest that what is so named is an active attitude or disposition to act which, in a particular decision of action, may be allowed to prevail and be manifested in the act, or may be disallowed. As this brings to our notice, it is not particular actions only which may be deliberated in advance and criticized in retrospect, but also such dispositions to act, as well as continuing purposes and decisions taken in advance of any relevant occasion. A disposition to act, or attitude, concerns some whole class of actual or possible actions, selected as having a certain character. And a decision taken in advance of the relevant occasion or occasions is similarly something determined upon by reference to generic character; it is decided to do some or any act satisfying a certain specifiable condition, as the occasion allows. Continuing purposes are likely to be even more abstract and general, and more obviously so, having reference to whatever act or acts will contribute to realization of some desired end. But here again, the eventual reference can only be to consequences, though this reference may be indirect. An active attitude or disposition to act is to be allowed and enforced, or is adversely criticizable, only by reference to some character of the class of acts so favored or disfavored, and to that common character which is essential to their being so classified. And in the end, both what an attitude or disposition is a tendency to do, and what criticism of it is to be made, must turn upon some character of consequences, actual or expected, characterizing the class of actions which are pertinent. There is nothing else by reference to which an attitude or disposition of action can be specified, and nothing else by reference to which an active attitude or decision or purpose can be relevant to particular occasions of action, or can be criticized.

However, it is also of importance to remark that no act can be determined otherwise than as a *way* of acting, even when the occasion of acting directly confronts us; and the difference between the determination of an attitude or a continuing purpose, or a decision in advance, and the more specific determination immediately to do is one of degree only. Though any act is a unique event, and together with its consequences constitutes some unique causal series of events, the total actual character of it by which it is unique must always run beyond our possible comprehension. No act can be contemplated otherwise than as some generality, specifiable by reference to some character, simple or complex, of consequences of the fiat of willing, or of the circumstances in which the act is done or to be done, or of both of these. It is for this reason that doing may be a matter of habit; what it is that constitutes the *habit* of doing is something common to the habitual doings; and that which evokes the habitual response is something common to the occasions which evoke it. Nothing that we can learn to do, and nothing that we know how to do, can be other than something generic and common to particular instances of such doing. No doing of so-and-so on occasion such-and-such is intelligible as anything other than some generality, both with respect to the so-and-so and with respect to the such-and-such.*

For this reason, there can be no decision of action, nor ground of such decision, which could not be extended to some whole classification of possible like cases. And for the same reason, no deliberate act can be decided upon otherwise than in a manner which could be formulated as a rule of action, and — if the decision is justifiable — by a rule which criticism could accept as one to be adhered to in all like cases. And no act can be criticized, and determined as justified or not, except by reference to some explicit and recognized rule or in a manner which accords with some implicit rule which reflection may elicit. If any intuitionist should object to this (no contemporary intuitionist would, I think), saying that on each particular occasion there is an equally particular intuition of rightness in doing, then obviously his rule is a very simple one: what accords with one's moral intuitions is always right. If critique has any criterion, then there is a rule. There can be no critique of action which is not formulatable in terms of rules of action. It goes without saying that the rules of any critique likely to be recognized as such will have some higher order of generality than any which should merely generalize the decision of a particular and justified act as a precept of doing.

It is also important, for the interests of ethical critique, to observe that any intention, being a prediction, is subject to criticism not only of its moral worth but also of its worth as cognitive. It may be morally right or wrong, but in any case it is cognitively correct or incorrect, valid or invalid, and true or false.

There is one manner of moral criticism which holds the doer responsible only for the moral worth of his intentions and not for their cognitive validity as predictions. This may be called the critique of subjective rightness. It is

---

*As already observed, the circumstances of the doing affect the act done only as they affect the consequences.

this mode of criticism which is in point in the assignment of praise and blame and for determination of retributive justice. A second mode of moral critique would hold any doer responsible not only for the moral worth of his intentions but also for their cognitive validity. This may be called the critique of objective rightness. Objective rightness is the important consideration in determining in advance what it will be right to do — hence in all deliberation of action. We may also note in passing the sense in which cognitive correctness is itself a moral concern, in the broad sense of 'moral.' For a creature capable of distinguishing the cogent from the incogent, cogency is imperative, in any activity which is knowledge-dependent.

Both because of its involvement *in* the moral and for the sake of comparison *with* the moral, the critique of cognition should be considered briefly. There are two grand divisions of decisions which are consciously — and, it may be, critically — arrived at: determinations physically to bring about and determinations of thinking — our concludings and believings. The connection between these two we have just observed. Let us consider the second of them separately.

It may be that there are passages of experience whose content is confined to affective feeling; but if so, they are exceptional. Characteristically, passages of experience involve sensory or imaginal constituents having some degree of perseveration — appearances or pseudo-appearances, the presented or as-if-presented. Constituents having this character, which mark themselves off or are marked off by attention, have the more specific quality of the present-as-present or the present-as-absent. The present-as-present are generally distinguished by relative vividness, clarity, and the character of enforcing themselves willy-nilly in their perseveration. The present-as-absent are relatively less clear and vivid, and in measure subject to our wish in their perseveration. A content which is present-as-present is normally accepted as sense-presented. A content having the quality of the present-as-absent is thought of, entertained. The affective feeling which qualifies the entertained tends to be generically the same as that which affects correlative sense presentation, but that which qualifies the entertained is normally less poignant and intense.

A train of mental entertainment which is undirected and responsive only to free association and its qualification by affective feeling is revery. One which is in measure guided or directed is thinking (in the narrower sense of non-idle thinking). Thinking which is assigned objective reference, or directed by the query of objective reference, is representational and cognitive. Some cognitive thinking may have no presentational constituent; some has both presentational and representational constituents; but any thinking which lacks any element of representation also lacks cognitive significance. (That representation may be substitutional or symbolic is a complication which we here omit.) Cognitive thinking is an activity directed to the general purposes of concluding and of believing or refusing to believe. It is in this character of it that cognition is an activity subject to critique.

There are, in fact, two distinguishable modes of cognitive critique — one narrower and one broader, the latter presupposing or including the former. The narrower, directed to determining whether what is entertained can be or could be representationally correct and have assignable objective reference, is the critique of consistency, the formulation of which is deductive logic. The broader critique, directed to determination of the veracity of objective reference, or the nearest approximation to that which is attainable — a warranted degree of probability — represents what episte-mology should aim to formulate. Historically, however, epistemology has never got far beyond its first question: Can there be a critique of cognition? Can cognition validly be assigned objective reference? For this reason we choose another name here, and speak of the indicated mode of criticism as the critique of cogency.

That such a critique of cogency is required, and must be distinguished from that of logic merely, may be evident from two considerations. First, logical principles alone are insufficient to determine any truth or any probability beyond that the statement of which is analytic, and any falsity or improbability except that the denial of which is analytic. And second, it is not possible by logical criteria alone to distinguish sophistry from science. Sophistical conclusions may satisfy all the requirements of logic, even if ordinarily they do not. For example, to choose first the conclusion to be supported, and then to select, from among known truths, those which, when taken in isolation from other evidence, will support this conclusion as probable, violates no logical rule of inference. But it does violence to the principles of cogency and is sophistry at its best — or worst.

Any critique of action presumes the critique of cogency as antecedent, since intention is prediction, and doing can be deliberate, and so criticizable, only as it is guided by cognition. The critique of deliberate and physical bringing about similarly divides into two: the critique of prudence and the critique of justice. What relations, precisely, these two have to one another is a moot point of ethical theory. We shall not discuss it here, but considerations which have a bearing on it will be presented.

Any critique aims at determination of some kind of correctness or rightness, as against some correlative incorrectness or wrongness. Rightness is that character which all corrigible and self-governed activities ought to have. Affective feeling may impel, and the feeling quality of representational experience may incline, but cognition *advises* our self-directed activities and our decisions.

There could be no biological sanction, nor any other, for the peculiarly human and complex mode of response by deliberate decision, unless that manner of response were accompanied by a sense of the imperative to determine it in accord with the advice of representational and, particularly, of predictive apprehension — overruling, if necessary, opposed impulsions and inclinations rooted in the more poignant affective feelings which qualify immediate experience of the here and now. Emotive feeling and the sense of the imperative are, thus, antithetic.

To conduct oneself so as to bring about that which, as cognitive prediction advises, will be realized with the quality of the undesirable is perverse. Deliberately to decide without calling upon the advice of cognition is gratuitously stupid. And to decide in a manner which is heedless of cognitive advice at hand is silly. To be rational in self-directed activity is to conduct oneself in that manner whose only alternatives are to be silly or perverse or needlessly dense. A rational being is one who is capable of deliberate decision and recognizes it as imperative to conduct himself by the advice of cognition, giving it precedence over his affective impulsions and inclinations. Correlatively, every rational being acknowledges critique of what he ought and ought not to do. To repudiate such imperatives would be to decide deliberately that deliberation is pointless and should not rule our decisions; to take it as rationally imperative to believe that there are no rational imperatives; to refuse, on principle, to acknowledge any principles — in short, to make oneself out to be intellectually contrary or inane or unnecessarily witless, and to prove it by pragmatic self-contradiction. The only consistent cynic would be one who believes whatever he wishes to, and for no reason, and whose assertions are made simply for the emotive satisfaction of hearing himself talk.

The basic imperative is, thus, simply that of governing oneself by the advice of cognition, in contravention, if need be, to impulsions and the inclinations of feeling. And this imperative can be avoided only by the incapacity to deliberate and make decisions. This most comprehensive imperative of rationality may be called the Law of Objectivity: So conduct your deliberate activities as to conform them to the objective actualities cognitively signified by your representational experience, and not by reference to any impulsion or solicitation exercised by the affective quality of experience as felt. Inasmuch as deliberate activity in general is something engaged in for the sake of its possible effect upon the future, this Law of Objectivity may be otherwise put: Conduct yourself, with reference to those future eventualities which cognition advises that your activity may affect, as you would if the effects of it were to be felt, at this moment of decision, with the poignancy of the here and now realized, instead of the less poignant feeling which qualifies representation of the future and possible.

If this manner of discussing the rationally imperative should suggest some biological sanction as final, that suggestion is not here intended. Plainly there is such a sanction, rooted in the natural capacities of the human animal and the natural circumstances of human living, and any supernatural sanction would be gratuitous. But question can be raised about the authority of biological sanctions. I take it to be a fact that the human sense of the valid and invalid, right and wrong, refuses to be coerced even by the cosmic process. If that be fatuous rebellion against the inexorable, so be it: I would delineate it as I seem to find it. If the considerations adduced vaguely suggest an evolutionary explanation of our normative apprehensions, that may be intriguing, but I would not use it, either explicitly or by implication, as an argument for the validity of imperatives. Instead, I would recognize that the basic imperatives cannot be argued for without *petitio principii*, but only by that manner of *reductio ad absurdum* of their denial which has been suggested. And that mode of argument makes its point only by drawing attention to the fact that he who denies nevertheless assumes what he so denies in his denial of it, and otherwise makes no significant assertion. The contradiction is one between the attitude of assertion and what is so asserted, not a purely logical contradiction discoverable in the cynical statement itself.

The philosophic sciences are the sciences of critique; that is their distinction from positive science in general. It is the business of philosophy — over and above the delimitation of those ontological and cosmological categories which must be presumed in all the sciences — to elicit those principles which will be recognized, reflectively, as formulating those criteria which are immanent in our critical, but perhaps unreflective, judgments of our practices as correct or incorrect, valid or invalid, justified or unjustified, right or wrong. Antecedent to reflection, we have our intuitions — so-called — of of the logically valid, the epistemically warranted, the prudentially reasonable, and the morally justified. There is no external ground for the attesting of critique itself other than such "intuitive" acceptability. But the intuitions themselves are criticizable, by reference to their mutual consistency or inconsistency as precepts, and their adequacy for decision of all cases to which they are relevant. They are also subject to reconsideration in the light of any developing and tenative critique, as it moves towards its immanent ideal of a set of principles completely consistent and fully adequate for critical judgements over the whole field of practice to which it is relevant. Being general, its principles must be capable of formalization. The general process by which formal critique may so emerge, in eventually systematic and acceptable form, is what has sometimes been, and should be, called dialectic: it is regrettable that this term has been so largely vitiated by inapposite and doctrinaire usage. This process is not altogether different from that by which systematic positive sciences emerge from empirical findings, which likewise are subject to reconsideration both by reference to their mutual consistency and by reference to tentatively accepted generalizations of the growing body of scientific doctrine itself. In all his self-directed activities, man seeks to generalize his critique of what is valid, but remains unendingly self-critical of his acceptances.

As suggested above, the ideal form of any critique is a set of rules which, taken together, categorically subdivide the whole class to which they apply into those which are correct and those which are incorrect. But as also suggested, attainment of this ideal is subject to the difficulty that the whole class, to which application must be made, can never be given and complete. As is obvious, the only philosophic science which presently approximates to this ideal is deductive logic, which constitutes the basic critique of consistency.

In the form which currently prevails, principles of deductive logic do not commonly appear as rules but as formal analytic statements of "logical truth." (Rules are extruded and appear as "metalogic.") This fact invites discussion of the connection between rules of correctness, expressed by sentences in the imperative mood, and formal assertions, expressed by indicative sentences; but that topic must be omitted here. We must be satisfied to observe that, as nobody will deny, paradigms of logic operate to determine consistency or inconsistency of statements and validity or invalidity of inferences — and as directives for one who would adhere to the valid and avoid the inconsistent in his concludings and believings. For example, the formal assertion "If all A is B, then no A is non-B" advises "If any premise of the form 'All A is B' be given, the corresponding conclusion of the form 'No A is non-B' may be inferred," and "Do not believe any statement reducible to the form 'All A is B but some A is non-B'."

Any full discussion of sets of rules adequate to the purposes of a mode of critique would constitute a study by itself. Only a few considerations which are pertinent can be mentioned here, and so mentioned as to aim at clarity rather than meticulous precision.

Let us help ourselves out here by observing briefly certain sets of rules applying to more restricted areas of our activity and characteristically phrased as directives or instructions by expression in the imperative mood. The rules of chess, taken together, divide all possible moves of a chessman on a chessboard into two subclasses, those which are chess-correct and those which are chess-incorrect. If all the separate rules should be connected by 'and', the resultant directive would constitute the categorical imperative for chess play. (This should be turned over to the logician, for his ingenious redaction in the interests of economy and elegance of formulation.) It is to be observed that, at any turn of play, the player is categorically permitted to make any chess-correct move he chooses: any such move is right, and it is his right to make it. But any move which is not permissible under each and every rule (or the one combined rule) is chess-incorrect. The rules "forbid" each and every chess-incorrect move; but they do not "command" a particular chess-correct move. It is under exceptional circumstances only that the rules categorically direct just one move, leaving no permitted alternative. It would be found, on examination, that some rules are permissive, whether expressed in the imperative or the subjunctive ("may"); other rules "forbid"; and some are, explicitly or by implication, both permissive and "forbidding." Some also may be categorically imperative, *e.g.*, the direction for initial setting of the pieces.

The whole set of rules (or combined rule) is "imperative" only in the sense of directing confinement of play to the subclass of permitted moves, and avoidance of those not permitted. But let us reemphasize the different bearing of the rules on these two subclasses into which the adequate critique of chess play divides all possible moves of a piece on the board. In any given set of circumstances (at any stage of play), any one of the possible moves which is chess-correct may be freely chosen; but each and every chess-incorrect move, under this adequate critique of play, is at all times and under any circumstances forbidden. (Some rules, of course, may be hypothetical in form, the hypothesis being expressive of possible circumstances at a stage of play or generally.)

Other games — checkers and card play, for example — would show a higher incidence of circumstances in which just one move or play would be directed, with no alternative permitted. But any set of rules which should always categorically direct the one correct move would constitute a form of activity (if 'activity' would then be the apt word) *unsuitable for any deliberative and self-governing creature*: there would be nothing left for deliberation to determine, unless what it is that he is commanded slavishly to do. In a game like chess, the privilege of the first move would then determine the outcome. In card games, it might not — due to the element of chance introduced by shuffling, dealing, and drawing. But if the rules of a card game were such as to direct, at each turn of play, the one card to be played, the game would be suitable only for children and such others as are intrigued by the hazard of sheer chance, since it would still be true that the outcome could not be affected by any deliberation of the player. Only activities whose rules of correct doing leave some element of permission in what it is right to do are suitable for deliberative but right-minded creatures.

One might think of a different mode of criticism applicable in playing chess. Within the permissions of the chess rules, the player decides his moves according to his discretion, with the purpose of winning, which is the *summum bonum* in chess and other games. That is, the player applies, as best he can, such rules as he has discovered belonging to another and prudential critique, and directed to the purpose of a good life — so far as succeeding at chess may contribute to that prudential end. Such a critique of *good* chess playing would be something quite different and enormously more complex than the critique of chess rightness merely. Some fragmentary and hazardous directives for it have been compiled; but for an adequate set of rules to be possible, the game would have to be simpler than chess, or no thinking machine so far built would be able to determine correctness according to this intended critique of *successful* chess play. However, this consideration calls it to our attention that one mode of critique may be superadded to another, in the direction of a single activity or mode of activity. In that case, however, it will ordinarily be necessary to determine which set of directives takes precedence, in case of circumstances in which they conflict. In chess, the rules of chess rightness take precedence over the prudential directives. The aim of winning, by itself, might in some circumstances advise surreptitious moving of a piece between turns.

A rule for making sponge-cake is likely to be the recital of some sequence of directives, each expressed in the imperative mood, though obviously they are intended as advisory only. Moreover, there will be more than one rule for sponge cake in the book. For an adequate critique of sponge-cake making, all rules the following of which would result in sponge cake must be collated and connected by 'or'. (We may then call upon the logician to introduce economy and elegance.) But it will then appear that many of the directions are permissive, and sponge-cake making allows freedom of choice to the cook.

To revert for a moment to logical critique, we may note the following similar point. Although paradigms of logic may sometimes cultivate the impression that logic dictates the one right conclusion to be drawn from premises, that impression would be incorrect. It is demonstrable that, given any premise or set of premises, the number of validly inferable conclusions is indefinitely large and limited only by vocabulary. The conclusion to be drawn may be further determined by some other consideration, such as relevance to a matter in question, and hence by some reference to some

But in inferring, the rules of logic take precedence over any other dictate.

Chess and sponge cake are things we can take or leave. Their rules determining correctness are imperative for the activities concerned with them, but such concern is not itself imperative.The rules in question have, accordingly, the character of what Kant called "hypothetical imperatives." But concern for consistency in supposition and belief, for validity in inference, and for cogent determination of beliefs according to the weight of the evidence is not avoidable for the animal that thinks deliberately — nor is determination of his physical doing according to the advice of cognitive prediction, or the end of attaining a good life, or justice in the social order in which he lives. These are not matters with which any human can concern himself or not, as he chooses. The rules of the critique of consistency, of cogency, of prudence, and of justice are for him categorical — in the sense which is correlative with 'hypothetical' above: the activities whose correct determination is the desideratum of these modes of criticism are activities he cannot avoid nor rationally fail to deliberate. Kant classified the rules of prudence as "hypothetical" because he conceived that morality is a matter of motivations, not of what is deliberately brought about, and also thought that for every morally significant act, there is one and only one decision which moral principles permit. And although he admitted that the prudential concern for happiness is psychologically unavoidable, he could not recognize it as "categorical" and "necessary," because he conceived it to contravene the one right motive. I class the imperatives of prudence as "categorical" because I disagree with each and all of these Kantian conceptions.

The bearing of the above suggestions upon ethics is, of course, a complex matter, involving much which has not been touched upon here. But I think we can, in the light of the above, define 'moral' in 'moral principle' and correlative contexts. This is obviously something different and narrower than the sense in which whatever is correct, according to any indispensable mode of critical judgment, represents a dictate of the moral kind. To delineate this narrower meaning of 'moral', I think we should, first, recognize that, strictly, its concern is exclusively with what is physically initiated and does not extend to any activity so far as that activity has no physical consequences. We can then define it by reference to the status of such moral critique. The moral critique is that whose rules take precedence in case of conflict with any other rule of doing. That is the sense in which even moral egoists intend the term 'moral': they are egoists by believing that it is the rules of prudence which so take precedence. But whatever one's theory of morals, and whatever set of rules one acknowledges as taking precedence in the correct determination of our doing, it will be in point to observe that application of the rules of this moral critique to our actions does not preclude coincident application of the directives of some other critique also. Unless one be a Kantian, moral rightness does not dictate disregard of the prudential; the attitude of obedience ot the moral law, giving it precedence over any other concern in case of conflict, does not dictate every moral act, leaving no alternatives to be otherwise determined, and precluding every other end as morally oblique.

It is another question, however, how rules of moral action, as physical bringing about, stand related to those of correct thinking and believing. Is it ever right to believe without cognitive justification, or to conclude otherwise than by the weight of the evidence? Obviously this question is confused to start with. Does 'right' mean 'morally justified' or 'cognitively justified'? On the latter interpretation, the question answers itself: the rules of cogency never justify incogency. But if we attempt the former interpretation, then the next question is: Can any rule of thought conflict with any mode of decision physically to bring about? Strictly, no. But cognitive beliefs are *advice* of doing. I think that the intended point of the question is as follows: Is it ever justified to allow oneself incogent belief in order to reinforce the affective inducement to some otherwise desirable mode of action? Or is it ever justified, confronting an imperative to do that which violates the interest of some subordinate but unavoidable concern, to comfort oneself by feigning their compatibility? Should the *interest* of cogency be subordinate to the *interest* of right doing? I see no authority by which one of us could answer such questions for another. According to my own conviction, the rules of cogency cannot be subordinate to any other. But to say that they take precedence over rules of moral action would be inaccurate. Strictly, no rule of cogency can conflict with any rule of doing: cogency advises action by prediction of its effects, but cannot categorically dictate action. And, plainly, we shall hope to be able to do what we ought without any noble sophistry.

The Ground and Nature of the Right
(SELECTED PASSAGES)

In all the world and in all of life there is nothing more important to determine than what is right. Whatever the matter which lies before us calling for consideration, whatever the question asked or the problem to be solved, there is some settlement of it which will meet the situation and is to be sought as well as various other ways in which it might be fronted which would fail to satisfy the requirements. Otherwise the issue would be unreal or else insoluble; either no consideration would be called for except to clear away our own confusions, or else no consideration we could give would avail us anything. Wherever there is a decision to be made or any deliberation is in point, there is a right determination of the matter in hand which is to be found and adhered to, and other possible commitments which would be wrong and are to be avoided. To say that a thing is right is simply to characterize it as representing the desiderated commitment or choice in any situation calling for deliberate decision. What is right is thus the question of all questions; and the distinction of right and wrong extends to every topic of reflection and to all that human self-determination of act or attitude may affect. . . .

It would be a little incredible — would it not — that the various ways in which men have applied these same terms, "right" and "wrong," should have no part of their significance which is common, and that there are no mutual implications between right believing and concluding, right valuing, and right doing; or between right pursuit of personal ends and right conduct toward our fellows. Already, we have suggested such a common connotation included in the various more specific senses of "right" and "wrong"; the significance of a desiderated commitment in any matter to be decided. The field of judgment of right and wrong extends to whatever is subject to human deliberation or calls for decision. And a meaning which is thus general is not thereby ambiguous, even when it is inexplicit or stands in need of elucidation. We can hope for any needed clarification, and anticipate that if it be achieved, something of import for more specific senses, and any relations which these have to one another, may be contained in that. It is in such hope that our further study here is undertaken.

Most frequently it is the moral signification of "right" as opposed to "wrong" which comes first to mind. It is the moral problems which are most commonly and most seriously pursued under that title; and one who announces "the right" as his topic is expected to speak of our conduct toward one another and of justice. We seem sometimes to forget that there is right and wrong not only about paying debts and keeping promises, but about adding a column of figures, or building a wall, or drawing a conclusion; about making an investment, playing a game, choosing one's vocation, filling out a tax-return, regulating our diet. And if it is true that any of these activities might be, under some circumstances or in some aspect of it, invested with a moral significance, it is still doubtful that the rightness or wrongness so attributed is one which answers to moral principles rather than to rules or interests of some other kind. We do indeed vaguely discern a very wide sense of "moral" in which it extends to every mode of our self-government and may significantly apply to anything we do and all we may affect; to everything concerning which there is any sense of ought or ought-not. Still that is not the usual significance of "moral"; the morally right is one species of right and cannot forthwith be identified with right in general.

It is indeed what pertains to morals and to ethics which is our main interest here. And it is also the distinction of moral right from moral wrong which takes the brunt of that skepticism which has been mentioned, and is charged with being subjective or emotive only, or merely relative to the cultural context, or a bourgeois superstition. But if it is the morally right whose nature and validity are most important and have received most attention, still it would be an oversight to proceed as if the qualification "moral" were simply pleonasm and moral distinctions cover the whole range of right and wrong.

It is, moreover, less clear than one might suppose just what area it is within which moral distinctions apply. One might expect that students of ethics would at least agree as to their topic; otherwise, how can they disagree? But examination of historic ethical theories reveals no such unanimity. It does, to be sure, come near to being generally agreed that rightness or wrongness of overt and deliberate acts, assessed by reference to their actual or expected effects of good or ill to persons other than the doer, is the major point of ethical investigation — though historic theories and authors could be cited to put even that in doubt. But if we ask what else, if anything, is essentially included in the scope of ethical inquiry, then diversity rather than unanimity shows itself to be the rule. We may — even must — for example, ask whether prudential action and decision of it, where any effect upon others is at a minimum, is to be included amongst the topics of ethics, and whether what is justified as adjudged on the basis of self-interest is to be taken as a kind of moral rightness, and questions of prudence as representing one type of moral problem. If we say "Yes," we are confronted with Kant who denies all moral worth to prudentially motivated action.* And if we say "no," we do violence to Bentham, who finds no motive save the prudential to which humans are capable of responding, and hence no content for moral assessment by any other standard than eventual self-interest.

That the prudential mode of judging acts is different from their assessment as just to others, must be granted if we admit that prudent acts may sometimes be unjust, or that some which are just contravene the dictate of self-interest. And if it be not granted without argument that the prudential assessment is a required mode of judgment, then it should be sufficient to point out that none of us could well determine what justice dictates unless we be able to weigh the interests of others — their self-interest. Conversely, if the doer's own interest be not already included in what just action must depend upon, the just man could hardly have any ground for judging the interests of others if he lacked the capacity to judge his own. If it does not go without saying that one ought to be prudent — as prudent, let us say, as justice to others will allow — then it should require no more than the question why we are so concerned to inculcate prudence as well as justice in our children, to assure the point that prudence is some kind of dictate, sanctioning some acts and prohibiting others, and that the distinction of the prudentially right and wrong is autonomous and distinct from that of justice and has some manner of its own validity.

The question of the relation between prudence and justice is an inevitable topic of ethics; and the questions of prudent behavior, apart from or beyond the questions of justice, constitute an inevitable problem of human life. Whether questions of the prudentially sanctioned as such are moral issues, would seem to depend mainly upon how one chooses to delimit application of the term "moral." To exclude them from ethics is possibly justified in the interest of the separation of problems. That, however, seems dubious: one could also think that such exclusion masks a derogation of the actual importance of prudential behavior or betokens an overweening inclination to the edifying. In any case, the prudential questions are problems of right conduct and, if excluded from ethics, must find their place in the larger topic of practical philosophy (or philosophy of

*Except in the rather far-fetched sense that temptation to do ill to others may be aggravated by finding ourselves in an evil case, and it is a duty to avoid such temptation so far as may be.

92

practice), concerned with principles of our rational self-government of action. . . .

Let us try to suggest what lies at the root of all the imperatives of our thinking and doing as the Law of Objectivity: So conduct and determine your activities of thinking and of doing, as to conform any decision of them to the objective actualities, as cognitively signified to you in your representational apprehension of them, and not according to any impulsion or solicitation exercised by the affective quality of your present experience as immediate feeling merely.

Since so much of what should be decisive of thinking and of action concerns the future, let us add a corollary: Conduct yourself, with reference to those future eventualities which cognition advises that your activity may affect, as you would if these predictable effects of it were to be realized, at this moment of decision, with the poignancy of the here and now, instead of the less poignant feeling which representation of the future and possible may automatically arouse.

Does this Law of Objectivity have bearing upon that last and most difficult question concerning justice to others,and the sanction of it as imperative? In this connection, we may do well to remember that the distinctively human mentality and the potentialities of it are hardly to be well observed if examination be restricted to the human animal as an individual organism merely. That of which man is capable, by reason of his peculiar endowment, can only be fully discovered by observation of him in society and in the history of the civilization he creates. Man is the only animal which *has* a history, the only species whose history is modified by his apprehension of it. Individuals of other species each begin where the preceding generation began, and their behavior is modifiable only by what they individually experience. But the generations of men begin where the preceding generation left off, profiting by the cumulative social recollection of what past generations have suffered and achieved. It is a basic consideration for the valid imperatives of individual human action that the possibility of that kind of evolution which man alone exhibited, and of that progressive amelioration and enrichment of individual life found only in the human species, is conditional upon the modification of individual behavior by social agencies. Indeed it requires modification of the individual mentality itself, as to its grasp and content, as an effect of social relations — relationships which themselves similarly evolve, and whose evolution is by the same instrumentalities. The peculiarly human kind of life is *imperatively* social. That fact is a datum for ethics. To do justice to that topic would need a book — and books have, of course, been devoted to it.

The basic imperative for individuals in their relations to one another, is simply the socially significant counterpart of what we have observed already: the dictate to govern one's activities affecting other persons, as one would if these effects of them were to be realized with the poignancy of the immediate — hence, in one's own person. The dictate is to respect other persons as the realities we representationally recognize them to be — as creatures whose gratifications and griefs have the same poignant factuality as our own; and as creatures who, like ourselves, find it imperative to govern themselves in the light of cognitive apprehensions vouchsafed to them, by decisions which they themselves reach, and by reference to values discoverable to them.

Perhaps we should divide this most general of moral principles into two. It has one part which turns only upon recognition of other creatures as being, like ourselves, subject to enjoyment and suffering. The dictate so derived may be called the Law of Compassion. And this same general principle of objectivity has another part or bearing which is relevant only in the case of other creatures who are like us also in their cognitive capacities and, in consequence, in the necessity of governing their own behavior by deliberation, and of acting under constraint of the imperatives of rationality. The dictate which is correlative here, we may call the Law of Moral Equality.

It is plain that the Law of Compassion extends not only to other humans but to all conscious beings in measure of that sentience we attribute to them as the capacity to find their experience satisfying or feel pain. Indeed this dictate of compassion is peculiarly in point in relation to those who are not our peers, but may lie within our power to help or harm in ways in which they cannot equally help themselves, or defend themselves against our intentions toward them. It applies to our conduct toward the lower animals. And it is also pertinent whenever our doing may affect humans who do not so fully realize the powers latent in human nature, and in those circumstances in which normal individuals may still not be able to exercise their normal capacities to the full. Again, and obviously, it applies to our conduct toward the immature, whose capacities have not yet fully ripened and been trained by the experience of life. This Law of Compassion must, I think, remain as an indeterminate duty to respect all conscious life for what it is, insofar as we are able to discern the nature of it as sentient. The question so involved whether every creature that enjoys and suffers, and not humans only, is as far an end in itself, is an infrequent topic in Western ethics. I shall not attempt elaboration of it here, or formulation of the law itself except as a general obligation: Recognize, in your action affecting any sentient being, that claim on your compassion which comports with its capacity to enjoy and suffer. Perhaps we shall agree at least that it is imperative, in any connection, to cause no useless pain.

The Law of Moral Equality shows, in some sense, the obverse of the Law of Compassion. It is peculiarly relevant to moral dealing with our full peers, and dictates respect for others not only as ends in themselves but as entitled to full self-determination of their individual action, to some privacy of decision, and to freedom from coercion in their decisions taken, so long as they bring no harm to others and accord to others a like freedom. But the morally more important implication lies in the fact that this Law of Moral Equality is likewise the principle of Equality before the Moral Law; the law that there shall be no law for one which is not law for all. This principle has joint implication with the fact that all self-government is government of *ways* of acting and by reference to statable rule. Both respect for others as our peers in self-determination under recognized imperatives, and the fact that self-determination can be exercised only be reference to some generality formulatable as a directive, have the consequence that no precept is valid and no mode of action is justified except as it is valid in the case of others as in our own. No manner of thought or action is valid for any of us except as, in the same premises of circumstance and evidenced fact, it is valid for all of us. This, be it noted, covers omissions to do as well as doing, since a decision not to do is a decision of action.

I regret to think that, for accuracy, this principle of Equality before the Moral Law must be stated in terms which will sound pedantic: Take no decision of action which is member of any class of decisions of doing all members of which you would call upon others to avoid. That is, I think, the intent of recognizing our own acts as right to do toward others only if we likewise acknowledge them as right when done to us. The particular points here are two: first, that rightness under rule is a matter of the classification or modes of acts; and second, that an act is right only if it falls in no class interdicted by rule. It is not sufficient that it exhibit *some* justifiable mode of action — be classified as doing of *some* sort, or acting in *some* way, which is morally permissible. What is essential is that it not be doing of *any* sort or acting in *any* way which is morally forbidden.

Our pedantic manner of formulation is dictated for the avoidance of two difficulties. First, there is the difficulty that a specious moralizer or a fanatic may elevate his selfish preference or one-sided interest to the status of a moral precept if allowed to do so on the ground of *his* willingness to see some mode of action universally permitted or made universally mandatory. Employers might so be free to accept it as a universal precept that wages paid should be minimal; and employees, that profits should be nil. And every bigot, content to see his particular bigotry become universal, could so justify himself in uninhibited imposition of it on others. But paying minimal wages is *also* expropriation of the fruits of individual labor and saving; and the imposition of any bigotry is *also* the imposition of private opinion on others — ways of acting which no employer, no employee, and no bigot could be content to see become universal.

Second, and somewhat similarly, our mode of formulation avoids those too easy generalizations often found as maxims but untrustworthy if applied without common-sense qualification, and hence dangerous in the hands of the injudicious or of puritanical rigorists. The classic examples are "Tell no lies" and "Do not steal" which, though hardly to be excelled for moral guidance in common practice, are out of place in dealing with madmen bent on murder.

No rule of action can do more than divide all acts to which it could find application into two subclasses; those which, under this rule, are permissible, and those which contravene it and are impermissible. But an act is wrong if it contravenes *any* rule of right doing. And it is right only if it contravenes *no* rule of right doing. An act is wrong if it is worng in *any* way; is any wrong way of acting. And it is right only if it is right in *every* way; if it is an act which in all respects is right to do. But if it be said that there are rules which categorically oblige some act, in all its particulars, then the answer is simply that this is not so. If it be a categorical moral command to pay our debts, what it commands is, "Choose *some* act, *some* way of acting, which will liquidate your debt." It is of some importance to observe that even the moral law leaves those who lie under its command some freedom of moral choice. Thus, logically viewed, the significance of "Do right" is "Do no wrong"; "Do nothing you would call upon others universally to avoid."

These principles, we may think, are basic for ethics. But lest the impression should have been given that, on the ground of them alone, we could straightway proceed to solution of all the major ethical problems, let us barely mention one such problem — or nest of problems — which we should encounter soon.

The Law of Moral Equality does not delineate the *content* of justice. For that, there are further facts of our common human nature which must be adduced, and further principles also which are hardly immediate inferences from those we have considered. For instance, the egoist as well as the social utilitarian can plausibly claim conformity to the principle of Equality under the Moral Law. In claiming prudence as the solely valid sanction for decisions of his own action, he likewise recognizes the moral correctness of others in so deciding theirs. He claims that egoistic conduct is *just*. If there is a basic principle of morals which he affronts, it is the Law of Compassion. But a Bentham or a Hume would be sure to counter by the observation that compassion is a native human propensity and as rational and "selfish" to indulge in as any others. It is more plausible to suppose that universal egoism is contra-indicated by the egoist's misapprehensions concerning the possibilities of a good life for anybody under conditions of uninhibited egoism. On that point, Hobbes seems more convincing; in such a state of nature life would be "nasty, brutish, and short."

But on the other hand, would life in a society of perfect altruists afford optimum conditions for individual happiness? Not, I should suppose, in view of our actual human nature. One of the major goods, of life is liberty to decide private matters on private grounds, without paternalistic oversight, and with the privilege of making our own mistakes. We even — most of us — cherish some privilege of competition with our fellows, within the bounds of our over-all social cooperation; and we think that allowance, or even encouragement, of certain modes of competition is essential to progress and conducive to the general welfare. But a mode of activity is competitive only insofar as individual prudential ends are put in front of any equal consideration of the good of others affected, and only so far as the success of one participant or party militates against the like success of others.

The content of social justice, it is suggested, requires to be determined in view of additional premises concerning human nature and human good which are empirical generalizations rather than principles of the type so far cited. There may be also, contained in such considerations, the suggestion that any positive ethics may find itself in like case on other points. In particular, it may be suggested that the grounds of the cooperation of individuals in society, for the sake of the common good, and the ground on which dictates essential to the maintenance of effective cooperation are imperatives for individual conduct, would be among the problems to be so probed.

If, in conclusion, we look briefly to the general character of any ethic which should conform to the general conclusions here reached, we may observe that it would be of that type usually called naturalistic, so far as it is classified by reference to the thesis that no act can be determined as right or wrong without reference to consequences of it as good or bad. Also, it would be naturalistic in its interpretation of good and bad as matters of empirical fact and as significant, at bottom, of naturally found qualities of experience. It would, however, have a character frequently taken to be antithetic to naturalism; namely, in the thesis that right and wrong are nevertheless indeterminable except by reference of rules or principles — principles themselves including reference to the good or bad as essential to determining what specifically they dictate. It would likewise be liable to classification as antithetic to naturalism in its conclusion that these imperatives of right, and the validity of them, have no other determinable and final ground than that character of human nature by which it is called rational. However, if a view incorporating both sets of these features can be consistently maintained, then what so appears is that ethical naturalism and ethical rationalism (if "rationalism" is the right word here) are not in fact antithetic but complementary. Perhaps they are antithetic only for a naturalism which connotes nature short of human nature, or for a rationalism which interprets rationality as non-natural and significant of some transcendent world.

"The Individual and the Social Order"

The moral you are expected to draw from the discussion of subjective right vs. objective right is that unless there be some discoverable property of particular acts, done or contemplated, which is the criterion by reference to which they are determinably right to do or not right to do, no imperative of doing could ever be applied to any particular act. And in that case, no such imperative could be meaningful, since there would be no act with respect to which one could determine either that this imperative directs the doing of it or permits the doing of it, or directs that it be not done. An imperative directs the doing of acts of a certain kind, or the refraining from acts of a certain kind, or both. Unless it is possible to *pick out* acts which are of that certain kind which the imperative directs us to do or directs us to refrain from doing, choosing to do what is right is a choice we cannot make in practice, and the directive so to choose is empty.

It is entirely possible to take as the criterion of being at fault or being innocent of any fault, in a given choice of action, the criterion of *thinking* the act chosen to have the character of the right to do. I take it that this *is* the criterion we accept in approving or blaming ourselves and others for what is deliberately done — with the qualification that sometimes we regard failure to think, or to think cogently, as itself blameworthy. Further, it is possible, whether it is judicious or not, and whether it accords in fact with the common signification of 'moral' or not, to adopt the convention that 'moral act' is to mean 'innocent act,' 'not blameworthy act.' But even if we take such subjective rightness — as I have chosen to call it — as the significant moral or immoral character of action, we cannot possibly take it to be what the word 'right' means in the statement, "An act is moral (i.e., innocent) just in case the doer thinks it right to do." This must be the case because if we substitute 'moral' for 'right to do' in this definitive statement, we shall have "An act is moral just in case the doer thinks it moral to do"; and that would make any inquiry as to what acts are moral to do an empty inquiry. To inquire whether an act is moral or not, when my thinking it so makes it so, is silly. There is then no character which some acts have and some lack which is the character called 'moral' about which we so inquire. Inquiring is a significant activity only when directed to determination of something which is as it is independently of what one thinks about it; and where 'being X' is synonymous with 'being thought to be X' there is no such character X which inquiry could disclose, or for the disclosure of which inquiry is needed. That X *is* so-and-so just in case it is thought to be so-and-so can be the case only where X is immediate to consciousness — an appearance as such or an infallible intuition. That rightness of an act is such an X is, thus, tenable only for the protagonists of the view that rightness of action is determined by an incorrigible and infallible direct insight; and on that view inquiry whether any particular act is right is supererogation: one always knows the answer immediately or else there is none. (Incidentally, what is currently called 'intuitionism' in ethics is not, of course, this conception of an infallible conscience, but the conception that the *criterion* of right action is intuitively apprehended. To know a criterion intuitively, and to know immediately what application of that criterion dictates in a given case, are, of course, two different things.)

If one be convinced that that character of an act by reference to which it is determinably right or wrong is one which it is rational to inquire about, then this character so inquired about is the criterion of what I have called objective rightness. It suggests itself promptly that the objective of any such inquiry is some kind of value which the act, as an empirical bringing about, may have. I have been at no pains to avoid that obvious suggestion; but we do not as yet have a right to it, since we have so far made no investigation of the nature of justice, which is, of course, a highly important kind of rightness which action may have or lack, and according to many ethical conceptions is the only kind of rightness, investigation of which is properly called ethics.

But I take it that our examination of prudential action — which is a much simpler matter — is already sufficient; and certain points to be made are capable of illustration by reference to prudential rightness. The criterion of prudential rightness of an act is its contribution to the doer's own good life of a value exceeding that of any alternative mode of action in the circumstances. That character of the act is a character of its consequences, and the question of it is a question of empirical fact — what consequences to oneself will actually flow from this commitment of action, and what value and/or disvalue will those consequences have as ingredients in one's own life. As we have seen, this question of comparative values is a question of empirical fact.

One who seeks to determine the prudential correctness or rightness of a contemplated choice of action seeks to determine his act by a criterion of empirical fact, future fact which he must, in order to reach the decision, predict. That is the question which determination of objective prudential rightness concerns.

Now the point I want to raise here — and I raise it here with respect to prudence particularly because I think the similar point will arise in connection with justice — is the question whether we shall be speaking judiciously if we say that a decision of prudential action and the act decided on will be objectively right just in case it is true that this action will contribute more of value to the doer's good life than any alternative open to him.

We are here well beyond the point where we can decide such a question by reference to common usage of the term 'right'; if we want to take the above convention for our own, that decision cannot be called wrong. But I take it that there are reasons why we should still be injudicious in adopting that meaning of objective prudential right. What we are seeking to decide in prudential decisions is future facts or events, and the measure of a certain kind of value they will or would have. It is the value so in question which stands as the criterion by reference to which we shall decide. But whether this act *satisfies* that criterion is a question of empirical truth; and with respect to it the best answer we can achieve will be one which cannot be guaranteed to be true but only warranted as more or less probable.

The question is: How *ought* we to decide such prudential matters? What does the imperative to be prudent dictate in such cases? Will it be the case that we shall have decided as we ought if and only if it is true that the act we choose will in fact contribute in maximum degree to our future good life? I take it that this will not be our decision. If, for example, we invest our money in a certain way this year, and next year it turns out that we should have been better off if we had chosen a different investment, I take it that we shall still say that our past decision was rightly taken if we can also say that all the evidence which was available when we made that decision indicated a larger probability that it would turn out well than that this investment which in fact would have resulted better if we had chosen it would turn out advantageously. That is, I take it that we shall say we made the choice to be made in the way in which it is correct to make such choices if we made it according to the *probability*, on the evidence available, that it *would* satisfy the aim of prudent action. We shall say, now that the later facts are before us, that we made a poorer investment than if we had chosen differently. But we shall say — shall we not? — that we chose correctly, if our judgment that, in all probability, the investment we made had the best chance to turn out well was a cogent judgment.

Is this the same as admitting that we did the prudentially right thing to do if and only if we *thought* we were doing the prudentially right thing when we did it? No. If in retrospect, we have to admit that there was evidence then available to us which, if we had considered it, would have indicated that some different investment would probably turn out better, then we shall say that we did not act as prudentially as we might, and our decision was not prudentially justified. We were somewhat imprudent in taking it. We *did* think at the time that our choice was the one most likely to turn out well. But our so thinking was not cogent. To think and decide cogently, and just to think and come to some conclusion, are two different things. The point is that there are criteria of cogency; and what it is cogent to think in any given case is independent of what anybody *does* think, and is determinable from the nature of the specific problem of such thinking.

You may have one further doubt: you *should* have one further question at least. So far as cogency goes beyond consistency and has reference to evidence which is relevant and available, cogency is a discursive character of our thinking, and one may be incogent, not by reason of dealing fallaciously with what comes to his attention, but by failing to attend to what calls for attention in relation to the problem in hand. Perhaps you say also, "Some people have a limited capacity for being cogent, and should not be blamed for an incogency they cannot help." I think we touch here a question of the very nature of logical truth, because one can say of consistency as well as of cogency that the individual capacities for satisfying the imperative to be logical are different and in none of us matches the ideal; yet there is no logical truth independently of the human capacities here in question. Time allows me to say only that relative incapacity to satisfy imperatives which rationality requires us to acknowledge is precisely that fact which obliges the distinction of subjective right from objective right. And the matter of approval and disapproval is the question of subjective right. Objective rightness is an indispensable concept; and it must be delineated in terms of living up to the imperatives we cannot repudiate. I grant that cogency, in any particular problem to be decided, is relative to the conditions of that problem and of deciding it. But if it be conceived of as relative to our personal and subjective limitations in meeting that problem, that will do violence to our very purpose in entertaining this notion of cogency, or any other notion which is normative in its significance.

We here touch upon that sense in which imperatives generally have their root in that character of man we denote by the word 'rationality.' Man is rational by acknowledging imperatives which he is capable of satisfying but, as a descriptive fact, is certain to fail to satisfy on some occasions. And this fallibility is likewise a universal human characteristic. And if it were not for his fallibility, the imperatives he acknowledges would not be imperatives but descriptive generalizations of his behavior.

As you will have noted, I should be willing to define this trait of humanity by saying that to be rational is to acknowledge it as imperative to be consistent, cogent, prudent, and just.

And now we must turn to the question of justice, which is the peculiarly ethical question amongst the questions of the critique of our practice — our deliberate activities — in general.

The three imperatives which we have, so far, sketchily examined are — I suppose — independent of the human social habit, in the sense that if we conceive of a normal man as living, like some Robinson Crusoe, without fellows, we should suppose him to recognize the imperatives of consistency, cogency, and prudence as pertinent to his thinking and doing, but to find no occasion for consideration of any imperative to be just. We should, however, recognize that no normal man — as we should use that term — could grow up to be even consistent, cogent, and prudent without the influence of human society upon his development.

In passing, let us note also that even a Robinson Crusoe with any roots of moral sense would be subject to an other-regarding imperative if he had a dog and a parrot whose lives were affected by his conduct. To note this is to observe a horrible shortcoming of the Western moral self-consciousness, in comparison with the Oriental. The Law of Objectivity calls for compassion toward every other sentient being, though it calls for respect only toward those which are capable of deliberate and self-critical determination of their behavior. If, then, we use 'moral' in the broad sense which I would favor rather than a narrow sense more akin to the literal meaning of 'mores,' we shall recognize that moral problems are not confined to those of justice to one's fellows.

I should like to preface our examination of justice by certain other suggestions (there is not time for anything but suggestions) touching the connections of this topic of justice with facts concerning the social nature of man. I should like to suggest first that not only is our moral sense as including the human sense of the requirement of justice dependent upon the human habit of group living, but it is dependent upon certain peculiarities of human group living as contrasted with other types of group living exhibited by other species. It strikes me that anthropological and sociological studies of human mores, in the literal sense, are prone to interpret these as simply an outgrowth in a species whose survival notably depends upon the habit of group life — the conditioning of man's individual tendencies of response, requisite to food getting and the other modes of adaptation essential to animal life in general, by the superimposed neces-. sities of group-life. That accusation is too vague to be tested, and I mean it as nothing more. But what I would suggest is that this overlooks the deep importance, for understanding human mores and human culture, of recognizing precisely what underlies the human moral sense. The most notable and most gratifying peculiarities of the social habit amongst humans are precisely those which turn upon what can only be described as the preservation of individual moral autonomy. No other species is capable of that manner of group life. But men are capable of deviation from this norm; and the manace of statism lies precisely in that fact. If the Russians succeed in their intentions — I don't think they possibly could, even if they were not actively opposed at all, though that is less than no reason for not opposing them — but if they should succeed, they would completely stop the clock so far as human progress is concerned, and probably bring about the extinction of the human race. If humans should survive at all it would be in the manner of adaptation of the anthill and the beehive, in which the individual is no longer individual but a non-autonomous cell in the organism of self-perpetuating hive or colony, apart from which it cannot function.

If I seem to digress in making suggestions of this sort, it is in fact because I think that we cannot arrive at correct conceptions of justice in the human social order if we overlook this indispensability to it of the autonomy of the individual as a self-governing being, determining his individual behavior by reference to his own critical judgment and acknowledging no final authority which can override his own deliberate critique in the light of the immanent imperatives which are authoritative for him because they are thus immanent and cannot be repudiated.

This is, of course, an ancient ideal, and very near the core of Western culture — one of the fundamental tenets of Christianity, and a root-concept in the long tradition of natural law and of government as deriving authority only from consent of the governed. But I think it has implications of a different nature also, some of which may seem opposite in their direction: unorthodox and unchristian even, by the fact that they imply the preservation in human society of individual competition as an instrument for the realization of social purposes. And that, I think, has a definite bearing on the problem which must have been in your minds already as a definite problem of any ethics which would accept prudence, directed to individual ends, and justice, more obviously directed to common purposes, as rationally imperative. The plain divergence, on occasion, of the proximate prudential aim from proximate social aim is what sets this puzzle of social ethics. How are these seemingly antithetic imperatives to be accommodated, compromised, or reconciled in an ethics which accepts both as rationally constraining? But here again, you will recognize a continuing problem of ethics, variously dealt with historically and, as I see it, never satisfactorily. How bring it to appear that the ideally just man, unwilling ever to prejudice the common aim for his personal best good, nevertheless does the best thing for himself; or that an ideally just society, never willing to sacrifice individuals in order to attain group ends, so moves to the realization of the most effective and otherwise ideal realization of the common purpose? That apparently impossible task is intrinsic to ethics, all the way from Plato's *Republic*, which succumbs to the ideal of an insect society with social castes as the paradigm of justice, to the individualism of Kantian Protestant Christianity, which leaves it a miracle which we must trust to the goodness of an unknowable God to bring about as the realization of His kingdom, and to the perfectionist ethics of idealism, which — shorn of its edifying and mysterious talk of Absolute Spirit realizing itself in history — merely exaggerates the importance of the goods of integrity (just as Kant does), recommending the sublimation of our personal sacrifices in the empathic vision of an immanent goal of the wholly rational community. But as Huxley said, long ago, puzzling this same question, it is difficult to see what compensation the eohippus would get for his sorrows in contemplation of the fact that his remote descendant will one day win the Derby. I think it just to shock this beautiful ideal by confronting it with the commonplace practicality that, in this old world as it actually is known, a community of Kantian holy wills, or yearning self-realizationists who forget to be reasonably prudent, will never win any historical prizes or inherit the earth, but merely, like too good children, pass to whatever reward there may be for them in some transcendental and unknowable realm. I do know say there is nothing pertinent in this ethico-religious ideal — men differ from the eohippus on this point. I do say an ethics which leans so heavily upon it is too other-worldly to be practical. And an ethics which is not practical is not

105

valid.

I would touch upon certain considerations which I think pertinent — each worth extended consideration, though they may seem to you remote from ethics. If rationality is to be practical (as Kant thought) its aim of justice must be practicable. And justice without prudence is not.

In the first place, the Absolute of idealistic ethics is a romantic fictionalization of the spiritual but practical fact of the human community of rational purposes. But these purposes end in values realizable in individual human lives; Fichte said there is no God save in the mind of man. I will not go so far, but will suggest that the only valid aims of ethics are predictable ones — the rest we leave to the unknown God who may bring about what we cannot predict and so can have no duty to work for. I translate Fichte into such concrete terms. There are no good ends to be realized save predictabel values capable of realization in individual lives. There is no transcendent Absolute whose glorious self-realization we can serve otherwise than by forwarding the aim of personal and individual good lives as those who live them may find them. The community has no central consciousness in which to enjoy or suffer. How horrid transcendental abstractionism may become, we should now observe when it is given the perverse twist which results from the unholy ,narriage of Orientalism and materialism: the individual life counts for nothing against the realization of the ideal community. For that, no individual sacrifice, whether of personal existence or integrity of personality, is too great. I say there is no value at which a moral community can rationally and practically aim save those to be realized in the component real lives of individuals. The community is a collectivity, and the abstract Society is an idol not even made in the image of any God which rational man can worship or could serve.

There are also other peculiarities of man as a species, some more and some less obviously connected with that rationality which is the root of moral problems and moral aims. There is the trait, seeming remote from this, that having hands, man is the tool-using animal. The consciousness of self, I suggest is largely vested in what the individual will controls. My body is mine because it so generally obeys my will and realizes my puposes. That is the embodiment of myself which I control; which realizes my will. And that over which I make my will effective is my realized self. The small boy envisages a big self as the locomotive engineer, governing this immense instrument of his will as it thunders down the track, or the aviator who swims up toward outer space on the perfected mechanical wings which, in his imagination, never fail him. The tool-using animal can so achieve a bigger self. And the self-realizationists have a valid and immensely profound point if they stress the concrete and practical possibilities for enlargement of the self through the unification of individual purposes with common purposes in a vast and complex and practically well-working society, in which he may achieve a life which is found good in contributing as an autonomous individual to a purpose realized in wide-flung organization of commonliving. The professional man, who makes his social contribution largely with no orders from others but by autonomous decision, is already, in Western society, accorded the great privilege of such a possible self-realization. With the increase of scientific knowledge and its pervasive and growing instrumentation by technology, the proportion of the community whose vocation becomes an exercise of autonomy continually grows. The contrast I would draw is with the biologically and instinctively achieved efficiency of the ant colony. The root of that contrast is in the government of action by imagination, knowledge, intelligence, and the realization of self-hood in the cooperative community of autonomous and self-respecting individuals, mutually respecting each other. The root is in knowledge and the imperatives of rationality. This is the progressive freeing of the human spirit. Hegel missed the essence of it by insufficient recognition of self-fulfillment as doing rather than merely thinking. He so left the way open for the historical antithesis of Feuerbach and the perversion of dialectical materialism.

Another distinctive human trait, so fundamental that it rates as biological, is the possession of language. And the peculiar character of human language, as contrasted with significant animal cries, is that while the latter can direct the attention of others to the immediately observable and directly immanent, human language can convey the past and the envisaged future as well as the present: not merely the presented but that present-as-absent which must be represented. It is so also that it can convey what is removed from presentation by spatial distance, and can communicate the merely possible and the needing to be done. Only by guesswork can we weigh how much this faculty of language has contributed to the fact that humans self-consciously live in a world as far-flung as the distant stars and in a present which finds its place in a march of time in which the here and now discernibly has grown out of its past and moves effectively into the limitless future. Only for man is the past real, beyond the presently felt reverberation and the future a definite locus of the desirable and that which may be planned. The first operation of cognition is translation of the now felt into signification of that which has a place and date in a limitless contemporary world in which all things grow out of their past and move into their future.

This in turn is the deepest miracle of the human social order. Man is the animal — the only animal — conscious of his history as a species, and by this self-consciousness affecting his own evolution and capable of directing it to his human values. Other creatures merely are evolved by natural forces they are incapable of comprehending. But man, by some capacity to penetrate the natural process, in measure controls his destiny. It is so that man alone evolves socially, and in a manner vitally affecting every individual human life, in a manner and with a speed which far transcends the limits of his biological evolution as an animal. If men today are biologically superior to men in — say — ancient Athens, that is hardly by natural selections, but mainly because his young have more to eat and are better spared the laming vicissitudes to which infancy in Athens was subject, by reason of comparative ignorance and the lack of control of conditions of life which that relative ignorance implies.

Each generation of other species begins where its parents began, because there is no social memory: nothing learned from the experience of past generations, no perpetuation in memory beyond the individual memory. For that, human language is essential. Man is the animal that remembers as a species and not merely as an individual. And the great instrument of his evolution, as a self-directed progress, is the social inheritance of ideas — the great traditions of agriculture, of technology, of science, of mores, of music and the arts, or religion and culture generally — by reason of which successive generations, with perhaps no heightening of the average I.Q. or other biological capacities, may still so immensely increase their knowledge and so rapidly extend the possible realization of human value and control of the conditions of good living.

The great instrument of what we call our civilization, which is so produced, is education, in its broadest sense, in which the knowledge and the wisdom man has won, as result of all past human experience, is passed on to each new generation. And a basic part of that is humna mores. These — as the governing institutions of the relation of each individual to his fellows — are the basis of the rest, the condition of individual learning. We are all of us born men and women of the Old Stone Age, with the same equipment of instincts and propensities of action. But the community seizes upon each of us at birth, ministers to our individual needs, girds us with the totality of acquired knowledge, and molds us in the image of its own spiritual attainment.

Oversight of this most impressive of all social facts is ridiculous, the puerile defect of the materialistic theory of history. The vital, the indispensable, factor in human history as human is not material. We live in the same old natural environment as all past generations. Biologically we are little different from our cave-dwelling ancestors. That our lives are so different, society so different, and what we eat and how we come by it so different, and our labor so immensely more productive and all individual activity so much more largely capable of its projected and desirable ends — the secret of all this lies in no material factor, but the spiritual factor of the cognitive and moral nature of man as a social animal. Strip the present generation of all their material trappings and reduce them to naked animals in the old environment, but leave them all their historically acquired knowledge and their acquired mores, it is not then implausible that men might come near to recreating our present human world in a generation or two. But strip the present generation of all faintest recollection of what has been learned since the Stone Age, and all their acquired habits of social living, and it is equally plausible that, in that case, the whole historical process would have, painfully, to repeat itself, and take an equal time. Man is not, as Feuerbach said, what he eats but — if we must pare down human value to the most exigent good of eating — man, at any moment, is what he is by his acquired knowledge and skill in feeding himself abundantly without the Old Stone Age labor of incessantly hunting for berries and digging roots, and chasing prey with a stone club. Economic institutions serve the basic and exigent material needs. And economic progress may largely pace and facilitate all other progress. But the secret of economic evolution is in the spiritual factor of the inherited and evolving idea-system of science and technology, and is no more than limited by any material factor whatever. Materialism is, of course, idiotic on the part of any self-conscious human — the perverse yearning of pseudo-intellectual eggheads to return to wallow in that aboriginal slime from which the human individual is removed by so many million years of progressive differentiation.

And what has all this to do with ethics? Everything. Ethics is man's explication to himself of that spiritual force which is the secret of the distinctive character of the life of the self-conscious animal. The moral imperatives — more largely the rational imperatives of consistency and

109

cogency in his self-directived and self-criticized mental processes, and of prudence and justice in self-directed doing — these are expression of the controlling directives by reason of which human life is what it is and what it may become.

On the one side, every item of what men are aware of as the world around them and the possibilities of their individual doing is something discovered originally to some individual in his individual self-consciousness. The only brains society has to think with and learn with and for perpetuation of itself as a mental and spiritual ongoing force are individual brains. There is no slightest conquest in human history which is due to anything but the thinking of autonomous individual thinkers. By language, what any individual learns may become a common possession of all. But it is by sorting and sifting of the social process that although individually acquired ideas are more frequently false than true, the true is elicited and remembered, the mistaken rejected and forgotten. But to impose the social authority of the traditional and accepted upon the spontaneity of individual human thinking would be, obviously, to stop the clock. It is by individual freedom of thought, and the respect for the individual in his own initiative and self-criticism, that human society has become human instead of an ant colony. Only the self-governing and self-criticizing animal is human and could be moral.

On the other hand, the human individual is human only by participation in a human society. The social historical process has made him what he is, and offers the only opportunity he has of what he may achieve and what he may become. Separate him from the social spiritual process, and he must return to the Old Stone Age, or to the level of ape-living even. He is what he is and may realize any value that he individually cherishes only as he meets the conditions of membership in a social order of individuals, cooperating in the pursuit of values cherished in common.

When we come to the ethical questions of justice, and the seeming divergence to the dictate of prudence, on occasion, from the dictate of justice, then let us not forget two things: first, that if one should ask "What is it that is most indispensable to the individual good of any human?" the readiest and most plausible answer must be, "The privilege of living in a good human society, profiting from its spiritual inheritance of ideas, and sharing in its cooperative institutions, preserved and furthered by its mores" but second, if any community ask itself, "What is it that is most indispensable to our ongoing life, to the distinctive character of the life we share, the source of all we cherish, and the hope of all further social achievement?" there the discerning answer is, "The fact that our social order is composed of autonomous individuals, capable of thinking and learning otherwise than by being told, and subject to their own self-criticism and the ultimate authority of their own self-government in action." If we suppress that self-governing initiative, we destroy that only root from which all that we possess has come to be and from which alone can spring any social advance to be hoped for in the future.

Only for short-term thinking could the contrast of individual prudence and social justice seem fundamental. But only by remembering it can the nature and the valid dictate of real justice be understood.

ABOUT THE AUTHOR

Vincent Luizzi

Vincent Luizzi is the Director of the Southwestern Center for Value Studies, which is housed by the Department of Philosophy at Southwest Texas State University. He is a Phi Beta Kappa graduate of the University of Rochester, where he received his A.B. degree, and holds a Ph.D. in Philosophy from the University of Pennsylvania, a J.D. from Boston University School of Law, and is a practicing member of the State Bar of Texas. He publishes regularly in professional journals in the areas of jurisprudence, ethics, and legal ethics.